Socio-Economic and Fertility Level of Chandel People in Manipur

Solomon Nungchim Moyon

&

Naorem Sharat Singh

RAJESH PUBLICATIONS

NEW DELHI - 110 002

Socio-Economic and Fertility Level of Chandel People in Manipur

Published by :
Sanjay Gupta
RAJESH PUBLICATIONS
1, Ansari Road, Darya Ganj, New Delhi - 110002
Ph.: 011-23274550, 43084725
Email : rajeshpublications@gmail.com
rajeshpubdelhi@gmail.com
Website : www.rajeshpublications.com

First Published in India : 2022

ISBN: 978-93-91139-41-4

Printed in India by :
Aryan Digital Offset
Delhi-110002

Preface

The association between the socio-economic status and various factors like education, agriculture, labour force, infrastructure, population growth etc. are witnessed in many past findings. More than 90 percent of labour force is employed in unorganized sector having no social security and other benefits of employment as in the organized sector in India. The socio-economically discriminated women are also facing various types of obstacles for employment. Having low educational status, many tribal communities generate their income mostly from agro-based, household based activities such as dairying, fisheries, small animal husbandry, handlooms, handicraft, social forestry and sericulture. Among the demographic indicators in the tribal areas, fertility could not be reduced to national level in India owing to its associated factors like low socio-economic status, communication, infrastructures etc. Even after seventy years of independence, India's fertility rates are higher in tribal areas 3.1 children per woman due to heterogeneous economic, socio-cultural and religious utilities. Sons are more likely than daughters to provide family labour on the farm or in family business and support their parents of old age, although there is some recognition that sons are no longer a dependable source of old age support.

Despite, no empirical study on socio-economic status and also their inequality has so far been conducted in most of hill areas in Manipur. Thus, the present study has investigated the effects of socio-economic and demographic factors on income differential, growth of agriculture and fertility level of the people of Chandel District taking the adequate sample size of 1071 households. It aims to examine the status of socio-economic and demographic characteristics in the district. The book embodies seven distinct chapters.

A brief but concise introduction with significance of study is thematically presented in the first chapter. The objectives have been clearly spelt out, as also the research methodology of the work. The methodology mainly consists of sampling design, sample size determination, data collection, data processing etc. It concludes with contents of the book. The second chapter is devoted to review of literatures relating to the present investigations. The previous findings are reviewed on the three primary aspects say relationship between income and socio-economic variables, relationship between agricultural production and socio-economic variables and relationship between fertility and socio-economic variables. The description of the study population is mentioned as the profile of Chandel District which has four sub-divisions - Tengnoupal, Machi, Chandel and Chakpikarong. It has factual indications associated with topography and socio-economic, demographic and environmental factors. It concludes the exploration of present field data of 1071 households according to more than fifteen elsewhere factors.

Under the caption of socio-economic determinants of family income, the fourth chapter is developed for examining the variation in family income with respect to various independent elsewhere characteristics. Using classical statistical tests like t-test and F-test, the income level of the population (mean family income of Rs. 12, 244/-) is observed to be significantly varied with various socio-economic variables. The variation in the mean income is found to be significant according to sub-division, size of female family member, number of literate family member, educational level, number of family members engaged in agriculture. Applying multiple regression models, five variables are again found to have their significant contributions on the variation in income levels. They are identified to be cultivable land area, number of literate persons in the family, educational level of male spouse and fertility level which is defined by the number of live births ever born to a woman. The fifth chapter is contributed to analyse the impact of socio-economic variables on rice production as an indicator of agriculture development. With the help of zero-order correlation matrix, the multicollinearity of various variables under investigation is controlled at r=0.05 and multiple regression analysis is carried out on rice production. Taking both wet-cultivation and shifting cultivation, the analysis is performed in isolation with Chandel district itself and four sub-divisions according to the interested explanatory variables viz., area of agriculture land, number of male labour, number of female labour, lobour cost, cost of fertilizer, cost of pesticide, cost of insecticide, cost of bullock/ tractor, irrigation facility, number of literate family member, and family size. The regression models on the rice productions for both cultivation types are also developed in each sub-division in particular and the Chandel district as a whole. Among the determinants of the agricultural production, irrigation is found to be most important variable in wet-cultivation in one hand and jhum cycle in shifting cultivation on the other.

The fertility level which is defined to be the number of live births ever born to a woman is found to be significantly varied with only four socio-demographic variables - categories of tribal/ non-tribal women, employment status, age at marriage, age at first delivery among the twelve variables of interest. However, in regression analysis, some socio-demographic determinants could be detected to be significant of fertility dynamics in four sub-divisions at different probability levels of significance. The important determinants are women's age at marriage, educational level, number of female child, child mortality etc.

Lastly, the findings of the present investigations have been summarized and concluded dealing with summary of socio-economic influences, policy implications and further research needs. It describes concise effects of various socio-economic, demographic and environmental factors on the variations in income level, agricultural production and the reproductive bahaviours of people of Chandel district in Manipur, the easternmost state of India having internationally border with Myanmar. Due emphasis has been given on the investigation of degree of influences of elsewhere factors on the variation in the said dependent variables by utilizing the multiple regression models in addition to classical statistical tests. The book concludes with discussion on the future scope of research on socio-economic development of Chandel district in particular and hill areas of Manipur as a whole in general.

Solomon N. Moyon
& N. Sharat Singh

Contents

Preface *iii*

1. Introduction **1**
1.1 General Outlook
1.2 Objectives of the Study
1.3 Research Methodology
1.4 Data Management
1.5 Chapters of the Book

2. Review of Related Works **19**
2.1 Income and Socio-Economic Variables
2.2 Agricultural Production and Socio-Economic Variables
2.3 Fertility and Socio-Economic Variables

3. Profile of Chandel District **46**
3.1 General Characteristics
3.2 Topography
3.3 People
3.4 Population Growth
3.5 Population Density
3.6 Sex Ratio
3.7 Literacy Rate
3.8 Distribution of Population by Worker and Non-Worker
3.9 Distribution of Main Workers by Industrial Categories
3.10 Surveyed Data Exploration
3.10a Distribution of Family Size by Sub-Division
3.10b Distribution of Agricultural Parameters
3.10c Distribution of Literate Family Member
3.10d Distribution of Educational Level of Couple
3.10e Distribution of Students by Educational Parameters

4. **Socio-Economic Determinants of Family Income** 68

4.1 Introduction

4.1.1 Test Statistics

4.1.2 Significance Level

4.1.3 P-Value

4.1.4 Confidence Intervals (CI)

4.2 Family Income according to Residence and Sub-Division

4.3 Family Income according to Type of Family

4.4 Family Income according to Community

4.5 Family Income according to Size of Family

4.6 Family Income according to Education

4.7 Family Income according to Agriculture and Allied Activities

4.8 Family Income according to Age at Marriage

4.9 Family Income according to Age at First Delivery

4.10 Family Income and Number of Live Birth

4.11 Family Income according to Child Mortality

4.12 Multivariate Analysis on the Correlates of Income Differentials

4.12.1 Introduction

4.12.2 Statistical Models

4.12.3 Multicollinearity

4.12.4 Statistical Inference

4.12.5 Dummy Variable

4.12.6 Specification of Variables

4.12.7 Functional Relationship

4.12.8 Hypothesis

4.12.9 Results and Discussions

5. **Impact of Socio-Economic Variables on Rice Production** 100

5.1 Introduction

5.2 Specification of Variables

5.3 Functional Relationship

5.4 Hypothesis in the Models

5.5 Analysis

5.5.1 Models of Sub-Divisions under Wet-Cultivation

5.5.2 Stepwise Models under Wet-Cultivation

5.6 5.6.1 Models under Shifting-Cultivation

5.6.2 Models for Sub-Divisions under Shifting-Cultivation

5.6.3 Stepwise Models under Shifting-Cultivation

6. Fertility Dynamics and Socio-Demographic Variables **133**

6.1 Introduction
6.2 Fertility and Place of Residence
6.3 Fertility and Type of Family
6.4 Fertility and Different Community and Religion
6.5 Fertility and Educational Level
6.6 Fertility and Employment Status
6.7 Fertility and Income Level
6.8 Fertility and Age at Marriage
6.9 Fertility and Age at First Delivery
6.10 Fertility and Child Mortality
6.11 Regression Models of Fertility

7. Summary **165**

Bibliography **170**

1

Chapter

Introduction

1.1 General Outlook

India has spectacular performance in the field of economic development since the introduction of New Economic Reforms in the country. In spite of it, the economic development in North-Eastern (NE) region including like Manipur has not been satisfactory. Without attaining regional balance development, the country could not achieve future growth and welfare. Moreover, the effectiveness of economic policy and the benefit of technological change depend on the availability of physical and financial infrastructures, human capital, topography, age structure, health condition etc. For example, social and individual benefit of engineers, technocrats or scientists in an advance country would be much more than that in an underdeveloped country. Various steps have been taken up to develop north eastern region including Arunachal Pradesh, Assam, Manipur, Meghalaya, Mizoram, Nagaland and Tripura. Sikkim was also added later on. The North Eastern Council (NEC) was established to act as an advisory body in 1971 and to function as a regional planning body. It was instrumental for the preparation of NER Vision 2020 document for integrated development of the region. Union government set up Department of Development of North Eastern Region in September 2001 which was transformed into a full-fledged Ministry of Union Government later on. Among the activities of Ministry of Development of North Eastern Region (MDoNER), the establishment of Non-Lapsable Central Pool of Resource

(NLCPR), North East Development Finance Corporation Ltd. (NEDFI), North-Eastern Handicrafts and Handloom Development Corporation (NEHHDC) etc. may be mentioned. Government of India has earmarked 10% of annual budget of all ministries barring departments having no scope for NER and departments with gross budgetary support is less than Rs. 10 crores.

NE states were also categorised as special category. This concept was first introduced in 1969 when the then 5th Finance Commission sought to provide fiscal facilities to backward states including NE states on the basis of certain characteristics of states which included: hilly and difficult terrain, low population density or sizeable tribal population, strategic location bordering with international boundaries, backwardness of economic and infrastructure and non-viable nature of state finances. Under this status of special category, these states got their plan assistance from the centre in form of 90% as grant and 10% as loan unlike this, general category states whose respective shares were 30% and 70%. However, this status was recently abolished on the recommendation of 14th Finance Commission. Moreover, look East policy and Act East Policy may be mentioned. In spite of all these measures, NE states still remain backward. Latest comparable data on net per capita income (at current price) shown by Statistical Year Book of Manipur, 2016 reveals that three year (2009-10 to 2011-12) averages of per capita income of only three states Sikkim (Rs. 1,09,949) Arunachal Pradesh (Rs. 61,132) and Nagaland (Rs. 56,542) were above the national level (Rs. 54,042). Within the N.E states per capita income was lowest in Manipur (Rs. 29,551) and followed by that of Assam (Rs. 32,597).

To speed up the development of these states, identification of specific problems and factors determining the development are highly necessary. Though these states have some common backward characteristics, they have their own problem in pursuing development programmes. Even in the same state different districts require specific development policies and programmes. For example, 9 districts[1] of Manipur state have different problems and require different approaches for economic development of their own. The policies and programmes for four valley districts – Bishnupur, Imphal East, Imphal West and Thoubalcould not effectively implement in five hill districts – Chandel, Churachandpur, Senapati, Tamenglong and Ukhrul. And again, Government of Manipur may even require different approaches to each hill districts.

Among these hill districts, Chandel is one of the underdeveloped districts in the state according to a certain available criteria. For instance, child sex ratio (ratio of number of female in the age group, 0-6 years to 1000 male children in the age group of 0-6 years) in the district was the second lowest (921) in 2011. In the rural area, the ratio in the district was lowest (911). The sex ratio of all age groups in different districts of the state revealed that the ratio was lowest in Chandel (933), the highest being Churachandpur (975). Percentage distribution of households by source of drinking water in Manipur in 2011 census revealed that percentage of household having tap water facility in the districts was only 19.2% which was the lowest among the hill districts. The percentage of household having septic tank facility in the district was the second lowest in the state, the lowest (10.0) being in Tamenglong. Annual average growth in establishment and employment in 2005 over 1998 (excluding crop production and plantation) revealed that the growth was only 3.40% which was the lowest among the hill districts. The highest was in Churachandpur (13.11%). Moreover, this was the only district in the state which showed negative growth in employment while in the case of Churachandpur, the growth was 8.95%. Moreover, Chandel is the district where highest number of tribes resides in the state. The ranks of Chandel district in respect of percentage of urban populations

1. Present study relates to prior to the formation of 7 new districts (Kangpokpi, Tengnoupal, Pherzawl, Noney, Kamjong, Jiribam and Kakching) on December 9, 2016.

(11.63) in 2011 census, percentage of male literacy rate (77.78) in 2011 census, percentage female literacy rate (63.96) in 2011 census, yield of rice in terms of kilogram per hectare (2213.55) in 2014-15, un-irrigated area in '000 hectare (12.41) in 2015-16 and percentage of main worker (37.28) in 2011 census were third among five hill districts in the state. All these show that Chandel is one of the backward districts among the hill districts.

Thus, the present study attempts to examine the determinants of socio-economic and fertility differential of Chandel People. Located in the South – East corner of the state, Manipur, Chandel district has an area of 3313 sq. km. and population of 1,44,182 in 2011 census. The district comprises 16.49% of the total hill area and 14.84% of the total area of Manipur. And it shares 5.05% of the total state population and 11.80% of total hill population. The success in implementing government policies depends not only on physical, financial and other economic elements but also on social factors because economic factors are influenced by social factors. For example, saving and investment are very important for economic development but rate of saving and investment depends, apart from economic factors, on the growth of population, birth rate, morbidity, dependency ratio of the population, saving habit, educational level, social tension and social and cultural activities of the people of an economy.

Measurement of economic development has been controversial one since the publication of UNDP's Human Development Report (1990). The report under the leadership of Mahbub W. Haq and Inge Kaulhad suggested a human development index (HDI) to measure this level of development. HDI has three components firstly, longevity of life as measured by the life expectancy at birth; secondly, knowledge which is measured by the weighted average of the adult literacy (with weight 2/3) and mean year of schooling (with weight 1/3) and thirdly, standard of living as measured by the real per capita income at purchasing power parity in US dollars.

Logarithm value of income is used to reflect diminishing

marginal utility to higher incomes. HDI is calculated by taking a simple average of these three indicators. In spite of the concept has widely been used, the old concept, per capita cannot be rejected altogether. Ray (2001) referring to many economists says "The creation of composites from such fundamentally different indicators as life expectancy and literacy is a bit like adding apples and oranges. At the same time, the apparent narrow perspective of main stream economist, with its hard-nosed focus as per capita income as a summary statistic of development, may not be too out of line. It is arguable that although taking a wider and multi-dimensional view of development is conceptually correct, per capita GDP still acts as a fairly good proxy for most aspects of development. For instance, it can be argued that rising income level ultimately and inevitably translate into better health, nutrition, and education standards in a population. The point of this section is not to discredit human development, but only to show that we must not necessary swing our opinions to other extreme and disregard per capita income altogether"[2].

Since HDI is calculated by taking simple average of three components of it (that is life expectancy, attainment of literacy and educational level and per capita income (PCI)) equal weight that is, one is given to each component. Such equal weight is illogical because PCI has more influenced on prosperity of people than other two components. Moreover, considering the present trends of using unfair means in examinations, the very meaning of HDI may not be attained if education attainment in Chandel is used in the calculation of HDI. The educational attainment through unfair means would not bring proper development of the society as implied in HDI. Moreover, calculation of life expectancy in statistically underdeveloped area is generally almost impossible as data

2. Ray, Debraj (2001), Development Economics, Oxford University Press. pp. 27-32. Ray refers this opinion to Anand and Harris (1994), Aturupane, Glewwe and Isenman (1994), Desai (1991), Naqvi (1995), Srinivasan (1994) and Streeten (1994).

on mortality which is very much required for construction of life table is almost minimal. In such cases, model life table is generally used. Even in using model life tables, population by age grouped data for two censuses are required. Such data is not available for Chandel district in published form. In view of the above line of reasoning the present study uses per capita income to measure development. Though there are many development indicators, per capita income is one of the most important indicators. Raising wellbeing and social capabilities much depend on the rising of per capita income. No doubt, mere raising of income without reduction in inequalities, the desire goal of wellbeing may not be attained. But without high income equal distribution for wellbeing is hardly possible. When people talk about development, automatically they have in their mind an economy in which people are well fed, well clothe, well educated, and ensured the availability of entertainment, healthy life, high expectancy of life. All these essentials of developments are closely related to income. For example, healthy life requires money for nutritional requirement, sanitation, medical treatment, doctor's fee, hospitalization fee etc. Per capita income is the ratio of size of income to size of population. To increase PCI, the numerator, the size of income has to be increased or the denominator, the size of population has to be reduced.

High income is very important for further economic development. Higher income implies higher saving and higher investment which are crucial for economic development particularly, in underdeveloped areas where mere technological change could not create the desire economic development. The higher benefit of technological change could be attained in higher income areas. These arguments justify the analysisof the socio-economic determinants of income in Chandel District, which is one of backward hill districts of Manipur. Generally, economic development of an underdeveloped area starts from the growth and development of agricultural sector. Role of agriculture has declined along with growth path. But the role of agriculture in the early stage of economic development cannot be ignored. In ancient time, agriculture was source of family income and livelihood. Agriculture gave major source of Job Avenue. Such role of agriculture is still true in backward and underdeveloped economies. Chandel as stated above is one of the most backward areas. Here, agriculture continues to be a source of family income except in the area of Moreh where international trade took place, though in small scale. Here too, number and role of original tribes of Chandel is very small. Because of their poorness or lack of capital, the major share in the international market transaction was taken by the outsiders, particularly non-residence of Chandel district. Moreover, there is a little scope of industrial development and development of tertiary sector. The district is a hill area where there is full of paucity of physical infrastructure (such as transport and communication, power), skill manpower (skill labour, entrepreneur, engineer, technocrats), financial infrastructure (such as banking and other financial institutions) etc. As a result of this the development of other sectors in the district economy may be attained through the growth and development of agriculture.

Distribution of main workers by industrial category in 2011 census revealed that 65% of main workers were engaged in agriculture in Chandel district while 74% of main workers worked in agriculture in hill districts. Further break up showed that out of the total main male workers 53.84% and 3.93% workers were employed as cultivators and agricultural labours in Chandel district while the corresponding figures in the total hill districts were 66.00 and 2.64 respectively. In the case of female, out of the total main female workers 70.35% and 7.30% workers worked as cultivators and agricultural labourers respectively in Chandel while the corresponding figures in total hill districts were 78.60% and 3.84%. Though the percentage of main worker engaged in agriculture in Chandel district is lower than that of the total hill districts, workers in the district still preponderantly depend on agriculture. This is true in the case of female worker. It is not only the major source of income and employment but it is also one of the sources of capital for tiny industries and pity businesses. Since the households have little access to banking and financial institutions and other source of borrowing facilities, they have to fall back on it for any small capital requirement of any ventures.

Shortage of agricultural production, particularly food production is generally agreed as a cause of inflation and poverty. Fall in food grain production raises price level of it which creates problem to poor people in gathering their require foods. The increase in food prices is also one of the main causes of increase in the wage of industrial worker which again leads to increase in the price of industrial production too. The foodgrain price affects not only industrial workers but also agricultural labourers and small and tiny farmers who cannot produce sufficient food. Thus, the decline in foodgrain production is a source of increase in poverty. Agriculture also helps in economic integration. Increase in agricultural production would enable some members of the household to participate in international trade at Moreh by giving small capital. Base on the above reasons, the present study focuses on agriculture particularly rice which is the major crop in the district as well as in the state. There is large scope intensive and extensive rice cultivation. Consumption of fertiliser per hectare is low as compared to those of other districts. For example, consumption of chemical fertilisers in the district was only 15.31 kg per hectare in 2015-16 while it was 17.63 kg per hectare in the total of hill districts. Similarly, consumption of pesticide has also been low. Moreover, agricultural production could be increased through extensive cultivation as there is plenty of cultivable land. If the people of the district have intension to extend their cultivation, production could be increased considerably. The justification for not extending their cultivation to the extent of expectation is that income derived from agriculture is very low as compared to pity business. But if modern technology is used and proper cultivation is adopted there could be high prospects of increase in the production of rice. The use of modern inputs (chemical, fertilizers and pesticides) and technologies and extension of cultivation for the increase of rice production depend on the socio-economic factors of the people of Chandel district. For example, the use of chemical fertilizers much depends on the knowledge of farmer which again depends on the literacy level and the level of education of the people. Therefore, the present study also attempts to identify the socio-economic determinants of rice production in the district.

Economic development also much depend on the growth of population. The interaction between economic growth and growth of population determines the economic development and standard of living of the people. High population growth has been one of the major concerns of any economy, particularly in developing economies. The study on the impact of population growth on an economy can be traced back to Malthus Theory of Population which states that human population grows exponentially while food production grows at an arithmetic rate. The combination of these two simultaneous growth rates would have resulted to no resource to survive. So, preventive and positive checks are required. In simple language, Malthus Theory of Population says that population growth has negative effect on the economy or per capita income. The negative view of population growth can also be seen in Harrod-Domar model of growth. The model says that the growth rate of national income equal to the savings rate divided by the capital-output ratio (y=s/c). This reveals that to increase higher growth rate of income, savings rate is to be increased which in turn requires to lower consumption. This has the implication of the necessity of lowering the growth rate of population. On the other hand, the higher growth rate can be achieved by increasing productivity of capital (by lowering C) which shows the necessity of lowering population growth rate so that per capita be increased. However, it may be noted that the model emphasised on saving assuming fixed productivity of capital. Per capita income grows at the rate defined by the difference between growth rate (s/c) of income and growth rate of population (n)." This simple formula is famous and has been frequently invoked to justify certain policies in over-populated less-developed countries."[3]

"Thus increased population growth has negative level effects in the standard growth models.... In the Harrod-Domar model, the effect is resoundingly negative, because population growth has no redeeming features, such as increasing the productivity of capital when more labour is available. In the Solow model, this redeeming feature is partially present. An increase in the population growth rate both increases the demands on the national cake and expands the ability of capital to produce the national cake. The net effect on long-run per capita growth rate is zero. Nevertheless, the level of per capita income at any given point in time is lowered. This comes from the assumption in the Solow model that there are diminishing returns to every input ...."[4].

These pessimist views of population were rejected by Simon (1971) and Boserup (1981). In their opinion it is not true that all people are unproductive. On the supply side, the increase in population gives birth to innovations. They are not just labourers but they are also innovators. To say in other words, technological progress is endogenous and hence, agriculture production could be increased to match with the size of population and the consequence of it may not be in the direction of Malthus who believed in the emergence of famine and war due to the interaction between food production and population growth. This supply side view was given by Simon. Boserup, on the other hand, gave demand side view. Population pressure on scarce resource encourages human society to innovate technology. She gave empirical evidence that countries with high density of population have more irrigation, use of more chemical fertilizer and practice multiple cropping. After surveying the empirical studies on the effect of population growth on the per capita income Peterson (2017)

3. Basu, Kausik (2000), Analytical Development Economics—the less Developed Economy Revisited; Oxford University Press, P. 45.
4. Ray, Debraj (2001), Op.cit., P. 330.

concludes "... the effect of population growth as per capita economic growth will probably remain highly country specific..."[5] Kelley (1988)[6] reviewed literatures that assessed consequence of population in underdeveloped countries. He observed the negative and positive effects of population growth but he was impressed by the statement made by the Robert S. McNamara, then president of World Bank, who compared population growth with nuclear war. Thus, existing literature does not give clear cut picture about the relation between population growth and economic development[7].

The increasing population can be used productively only when they are employed with proper skill and complementary capital and infrastructure required. But the scope of such optimistic view is very limited in such area as Chandel where there is little scope of irrigation and innovation. Scope of irrigation area is limited because of hilly topography and scope of innovation is limited by low level of knowledge in term of training and level of education. Though there is vast area of land the scope of using modern inputs is very limited because of hilly topography and low level of education. In such area high growth rate of population creates pressure on limited resources, reduces private and public capital formation, diverts valuable funds from capital formation to consumptions. Without concomitant factors, a mere increase in labour force will not be helpful to the economic development. The above argument shows that the growth of population in the district should be checked. The growth of population has three components – fertility, mortality and migration. Among these components fertility is the major component which is the responsible factor for population

---

5. Peterson, EWF (2017). The Role of Population in economic growth. Available at https.//journals.sagepub.com>doi>abs:9.
6. Kelley Allen C. (1988). Economic Consequence of Population Changes in the third world. Journal of Economic Literature, 26(4) : Dec: 1685-1728.
7. Easterline, Rechard A. (1967). The Effect of Population Growth on the Economic Development of Developing Countries. The Annals of the American Academy of Polity: 98-108.

growth. Therefore, the present study also attempts to explain the major socio-economic determinants of fertility. The study would help much in formulating policy programmes for the development of Chandel district by finding the key variables which determine the growth of income and agriculture and check growth of population in Chandel district. Importance of such study is also enhanced by limited number of such studies on tribal area.

1.2 Objectives

The present study attempts to examine the impact of socio-economic factors on level of income, agriculture production and fertility dynamics in Chandel district of Manipur. The specific objectives of the study are:

1. To examine the variation in family income with respect to place of residence and sub-division, type of family, community, size of family, education, area under rice cultivation, age at marriage, age at first delivery, fertility and child mortality in isolation and also in multivariate model.
2. To verify the change in agricultural production in response to change in area under rice cultivation, number of male family members engaged in agriculture activities, labour cost, cost of fertilizer, pesticides, insecticide, bullock/tractor, irrigation facility, number of literate persons in the family, size of family and Jhum cycle.
3. To evaluate the variation in the average fertility according to factors such as place of residence, type of family, religion, family income, source of drinking water, major means of cooking, type of latrine, age at marriage of wife, educational level of both spouses, number of son, employment status of family members, age at first delivery, child mortality, number of daughter, and number of children born alive but now deceased.

1.3 Research Methodology

This section explains the research methods used in the present study consisting of sample design, sample size, preparation of field work, data collection, data processing, the variable studied, definition of concepts used and data analysis. The broad materials and methods of the study are as follows:

Research question: What are the socio-economic factors influencing the variation in the income, rice production and fertility of the households in Chandel district of Manipur?

Area of study: Chandel district which is one of the hill districts of Manipur.

Sample size: The size of sample of the present study is 1071 households. It is determined by the formula, $n = \frac{\xi_\alpha \sigma^2}{\varepsilon^2}$, where n is the sample size; ξ, the standard normal variate value (1.96 say approximately 2) at $\propto$ (0.05) level; σ, the standard deviation and ε is the margin of error (taking the prior information through a pilot survey of 30 households).

Sampling: Stratified random sampling with proportional allocation.

Dependent Variables: Family income (monthly income of the family), agricultural production (average product of rice of the family), and fertility (the number of live births ever born to a mother).

Independent Variable: Various socio-economic, demographic, behavioural and cultural factors.

Tools: Pre-tested and semi structural interview questionnaire.

Analysis: Statistical analysis has been performed by utilising multiple regression models in addition to the classical statistical test – *t* and *F*

(ANOVA). Some secondary data like NFHS – figures, census figures and past reports furnished by organised agencies are incorporated in the case of discussion and interpretation of the findings.

Statistical package: SPSS (statistical package for social sciences) vs 23.

1.4 Data Management

Socio-economic condition of the district can be studied through secondary data or primary data. Since secondary data available for the district was very limited, primary data was collected. Primary data can be collected through census survey or sample survey. In view of limited time, money, law and order and topographical feature of the district, the sample survey was attempted. Literacy rate and workers participation rate are very important for determining socio-economic conditions of an area, like Chandel. Many studies argue that education is the optimal measure because it is very important for employment, income generation, information gathering, healthy living, and is critical for the use of health care system[8]. Income, on the other hand, is emphasized by some studies on the ground that it is used to purchase health care and prefer qualities of nutrition. Moreover, it is one of the major determinants of saving and investment for increasing of production[9]. But village wise income was not available and hence workers participation was used as proxy variable for

8. Christenson, B. A and Nan, E.J. (1995), Educational Inequality in Adults Mortality: Assessment with Death Certificate Date in Michigan. Demography, 32: 215-230 and Elo I.T. and Samual, H.P. (1992), Effects of Early Life Condition in Adult Mortality: a Review. Population Index, 58(2): 186-212.
9. Adler, N. et.al. (1994). Socio-economic Status and Health: the Change of the Gradient American Psychologist, 49(1): 15-24 cited by Hummer Robert et.al. (1998). Socio-Demographic in Adult Mortality: a review of Analytic Approaches, Population and Development Review, 24(3): 553-578.

income. The reason for this is that income is very closely connected with workers participation (more specifically with employment). It may also be noted that female literacy rate and female workers participation rate are more important determinants of socio-economic of any economy. Highest female literacy rate (97.54) was found in Laiyang village while the lowest literacy rate was found in the villages T. Sijang, Khumunnun, L. Boonjang. Similarly, very high inequality in respect of female work participation was reported in 2011 census. Molkon had the highest work villages T. Sijang, Khumunnun, L. Boonjang. Similarly, very high inequality in respect of female work participation was reported in 2011 census. Molkon had the highest work participation rate (93.33) and the lowest (0.00) was found in Songkong and Sarang Tampak of Chandel district.

In view of these wide disparities in respect of these two important determinants of socio-economic condition, the present study adopted stratified random sampling. There were 350 villages in rural area of the district, these villages were arranged in descending orders in respect of female literacy rate and female work participation rate. Ranks of villages were added to form a composite rank of villages. For example, if a particular village had 12th and 100th ranks with respective to the above variables; the composite rank of this village was 112. After finding the composite ranks of the village, the villages were again rearranged in descending order according to the composite rank. Then, the villages were grouped into three. In the first group there are 67 villages which fell in 1st to 50th ranks covering 2831 households. There were 228 villages having 11956 households in the second group which was found in 51st rank to 100th rank. The last group (that is, from 101st to 150th ranks) consists of 55 villages which were inhabited by 3146 households.

Conducting a pilot study of 30 households, the sample size is determined by the formula " $n = \frac{\xi_\alpha \sigma^2}{\varepsilon^2}$ " where n is the sample size; ξ, the standard normal variate value (1.96 say approximately 2) at $\propto$ (0.05) level; σ , the standard deviation and ε is the margin of error. The desire sample size was found to be 1071. It was computed on the basis of the pilot survey (Mean $\pm$ SD of monthly family income = Rs. 10,542 $\pm$ 8621) under 95% degree of precision with 5% margin of error to the mean family income.

A pre-tested and semi-structural interview questionnaire was prepared which consisted of the following main sections - house module, demographic module, agriculture module, industry module, livestock module, employment module and consumer-expenditure module. Section one dealt with the basic characteristics of the households; demographic module dealt with fertility, mortality and migration; the next module investigated wet cultivation, shifting cultivation and terrace cultivation; industry module mainly concerned with employment; livestock module showed the contribution of different domestic animals; employment module concerned with source of employment in different sectors of economy; the last module related the expenditure pattern of different socio-economic levels of Chandel people.

Since the district is hilly area which has the problem of transport and communication, it was decided to employ four male investigators along with the present researcher. In order to give clear information and idea, 10 days training was given to these 4 investigators whose qualifications were all graduates. Free and frank discussion was taken during training period so that they do not face any problem of the concept and questions included in the questionnaire. Moreover, a pilot survey was also conducted to 30 households in nearby villages and necessary corrections were made to obtain the above objectives.

The sample survey was conducted during the twelve months periods from the 1st August 2010 to 30th July 2011. The investigator first tried to contact village head or chief so that he informed his people to co-operate while interviewing them. Since most of the villagers were in the interior and far away from the district head quarter and also there were long distance between villages, the investigators were compelled to hold a night or two in the villages. Moreover, there was risk of facing wild animals in the night. During harvest season which starts from the second week of October and ends in the last week of November people used to go in their paddy field in the morning and returned to their home at dusk. Sometimes, if the field was far away from their home they hold nights in the huts constructed at fields. In such situations the investigators faced the problem of meeting with them. The investigators took the chance of interviewing them when they did not go to their fields.

After reaching the concern village the researcher used to contact the village chief or head and explained the purpose of the study and sought his help for full co-operation of the villagers. The villagers gave full co-operation and readiness to help. Most of them responded friendly. Exceptionally it was found some disturbances from the persons who used alcohol during late evenings. With a view to get the true information the researcher adjusted his time according to free time of the respondents. During the interview one respondent was assisted by another family member. In case of any doubt was seen, the investigators explained clearly and convincingly to get the true respond. After asking all questions in the questionnaire schedule, care was taken to ensure no questions were left unanswered. The unanswered or incomplete questionnaire was resurveyed as soon as possible.

Data collected were codified and processed through SPSS vs 23 to get the desire tabular form for different strata and sub-strata. To find out the causal relationship between socio-economic variables and income, agriculture and fertility, different regression analysis were done and test of significance were also examined. Selected socio-economic variables used in the present analysis will be explained in the relevant chapters again.

1.5 Chapters of the Book

The present reference book consisted of seven chapters. A concise introduction is presented in the first chapter. Here, background, problem, objectives and the methodology of this present investigation have clearly been spelt out. Thesecond chapter reviewed relevant literatures. The third chapter is devoted on the profile of the Chandel District. In the fourth section, the variations in the family income of the surveyed population according to twenty-seven interested factors have been analysed by using classical least square method along with statistical tests say t-test and F-test. By using regression models, the most influential factors on the variation in the income level of the population are also identified in this chapter. The fifth chapter is contributed the nature and pattern of the agriculture production under wet-land and shifting cultivation systems. It is specifically dealt with rice production and its influencing factors in multi-variate analysis with regression models. In the sixth chapter, the variation in the average fertility has been examined according to interested ten variables in isolation by utilizing F-test and t-test. The set of influencing socio-economic factors in the fertility dynamics was also identified with the help of regression analysis. The last chapter is the summary and implications of the present investigation. The effects of various socio-economic, behavioural, and demographic factors on the variations in the average income level of the study population, rice production and fertility have been highlighted. It has also concisely presented the overall findings of the study that have been described in the previous chapters of the book.

2

Chapter

Review of Related Works

This section reviews the studies relating to the socio-economic determinants of income, agriculture production and human fertility. These past studies are grouped according to three dependent variables viz., income level, agriculture production and fertility. The sequence of the review also broadly reflects the chronological order within each sub-section. The sub-sections start from income and followed by agriculture production and human fertility respectively.

2.1 Income and Socio-Economic Variables

Rosenz weig (1987) reviewed a number of empirical studies on the relation between population and economic development. The evidence suggested majority of observed correlations among population growth, human capital and economic variables were far stronger than the estimates from studies which attempted to find the casual mechanism among population growth, human capital investment and economic development. The methods used in and the finding of these studies were spurious in the sense that they could not establish a solid empirical foundation of these issues and the frailty of the actual evidence pertinent to the extreme. In spite of this, certain regularities were emerged from these studies based on data from the USA, Columbia, India, Indonesia, Malaysia and the Philippines and informed by models of household behaviour incorporating many of biological process associated with human reproduction and development. To mention a few (a) returns to investment in skills appeared to directly affect both the levels of investments in skill and family size decision (when fertility falls and productivity of human capital raised due to increase in investment in human capital); (b) early and prolong child bearing directly decreased the human capital of children; (c) difficulty in controlling of fertility led to decrease the level of human capital etc. However, the magnitude of these empirical causal relationships was found relatively small. Thus, the observed correlations among these three elements appear to overstate considerably.

Romer (1990), Nobel Laureate of 2018 says growth is driven by technological change. He further explains that in his model of indigenous technological change, the engine of growth operates in market place where intentional investment was driven by profit maximising behaviour of economic agents (entrepreneurs). Market or price incentive plays the major role in the process whereby new knowledge was translated with goods of practical importance. Technology is the application of scientific knowledge for practical purpose. Technological change was defined by him as an improvement in the instructions for mixing together raw materials. Technology has a distinguishing feature that unlike conventional good and public good, it is a non-rival and partially excludable good. His major conclusions were that rate of growth was driven by human capital, that very little human capital was used for research in equilibrium, that free international trade can speed up growth and that growth of economy requires more human capital rather than larger size of population. The most striking positive implication of his finding is that an economy with larger total stock of human capital would experience faster growth.

One of the most relevant studies on development for the present study is Human Capital Revisited of Becker (1994). He says education and training are the most significant investment in human capital. High school and college education raised not personal income not only in the USA but also in more than one hundred countries. The gains were generally larger in less-developed countries. Education increased not only income but also promoted health, reduced smoking, improved birth control knowledge etc. There is also a close relation between human capital and families. Families influenced on the knowledge, marriage, skills, values and habits of their children. There was large difference among young children grow over time with age and schooling because children learnt more easily when they were better prepared. Because of education there was closer earning of children and parents in poor families as compared to those richer families who could pay more for education and training. The negative relation between number of children and spending per child found in family level implies negative relation at the aggregate level between population growth and investment in human capital. Children of Japanese, Chinese, Jews and Cubans were well educated because they have smaller families. On the other hand Mexicans, Puerto Ricans and black families had not well educated children as they had very large families.

Long run economic development experienced by the US, Japan and many European countries was the result of the expansions of scientific and technical knowledge that raised the productivity of labour and other inputs in productions. He emphasised the importance of human capital and technology for the development of agriculture. In traditional society education was of little importance because farming methods and knowledge were then easily come from their forefathers. In the case of modern agricultural production system education has been of great value since it has helped in learning modern method of farming, including proper use of fertiliser, insecticide, seeds and other inputs. Barro (1996) revealed that the data from the empirical findings for a panel of around 100 countries from 1960 to 1990 clearly provided necessary information to isolate the determinants of economic growth and strongly supported the conditional convergence of growth in the globe. With respect to government policies the evidence indicated that there was significant positive correlation between growth of real per-capita GDP on one hand and better maintenance of the rule of law, smaller government consumption, and lower inflation on the other. Growth rate was stimulated by male secondary and higher schooling, by greater starting level of life expectancy, by lowering fertility rates and by improvement in term of trade. When population growth was high, the economy could not raise capital per-worker because a part of the investment was used to provide capital to new worker. In addition to this, higher fertility implied higher amount of resources must be devoted to child bearing. Fertility decision was endogenous as it declined with prosperity and female education. Life expectancy was proxied by health as well as quality of human capital. Education promoted growth as it increased the ability to absorb new technology. Female education enhanced economic growth indirectly by lowering fertility. Given these and other variables, growth rate was negatively correlated with the initial level of per-capita GDP. Lastly, he noted that the poor tended to grow faster than the rich.

Unlike most of the other studies which estimated private returns to education as order of 6-10%, Acemoglu and Angrist (2001) estimated positive external returns to variations in average schooling caused by changes in compulsory schooling laws in the USA. They employed OLS method and 2SLS method for estimation purpose. When they used data from 1960 to 1980, they found insignificant externality around 1% (mostly ranging from 1 to 3%). Adding data from 1950 the study brought about the same pattern with somewhat precise estimate. However, the estimation by using data from 1990 census revealed statistically significant estimates of external returns of 4% or more. This might reflect that the importance of human capital increased after 1980 and the larger estimate found in 1990 might be due to changes in the schooling variable in the 1990 census. The final caveat shown by them were: standard errors associated with estimates reported in their study "leads to confidence intervals that include external returns of, say 1-3%" which justified significant government subsides for education. And the estimates were raised by the variation in secondary schooling and not changes in higher education.

In view of investment rates in most Muslim developing countries were on average lower than those of non-Muslim developing countries, Salahuddin et al. (2009) has tried to find out the determinants of investment in 21 Muslim developing countries over the period of 1970 to 2002. Unlike other studies the study carefully employed estimations procedures. To control time invariant unobserved country specific fixed effect, fixed effect estimator was used. Difference Generalised Method of Moment (GMM) dynamic panel was employed to compensate endogeneity of the regressors. To check the reverse causality, Granger causality was also performed. The explanatory variables found positive and significant in explaining the variations in gross investment were lagged investment, growth rate of per capita real GDP, domestic savings, trade openness and institution development. Foreign aid and private sector credit were else also found positive significant impact on investment. The remaining variables – rate inflation, lending rate, human capital (proxied by secondary school enrolment) and population growth rate were found insignificant.

Nagarajan et al. (2013) reviewed extensively the studies on the relationship between ageing of population and economic growth and ultimately concluded ageing had effect on economic growth through three main mechanisms: consumption and saving pattern, public expenditure, and human capital. Their review revealed that the impact of ageing depended on the mechanism chosen. Negative relation between ageing and economic growth was found in about 70% of empirical studies that focussed on public expenditure. While no significant relation come across in 60% of empirical studies which emphasised on human capital and it was also found ageing was positively related to economic growth in those studies which focused on consumption and saving pattern. On the whole, mechanism appeared to non-trivial influence on the relation between ageing and economic growth. Moreover, the nature of relation was considerably influenced by the estimation method. Less sophisticated econometric methods (OLS and Panel) were associated with negative relation whereas likely positive influence or no significant was found with Overlapping Generation Method and Generalised Method of Moments (GMM).

Nwibo and Alimba (2013) tried to find out determinants of investment decision among agribusiness investors in south-east Nigeria which comprised of 5 states, namely; Anambra, Imo, Abia, Enugu and Ebonyi. They employed both purposive and multistage sampling technique. The collected data was analysed with the help of descriptive statistics (such as percentage, means etc.) and probit regression model. The dependent variable, investment decision (ID) was explained as ID=1 (effect on decision to invest) and ID=0 (no effect on decision to invest). The socio-economic independent variables included were age (in years); gender of investor (male=0, female=1); level of education (FSLC=1, SSCE=2, OND=3, BSC=4, MSC and above=5) of the investor; experience (experience=0, not experience=1); annual personal income of the investor (naira); household size (total number of persons feeding from the investor's plot/house); household entrepreneurial history (father/mother=1, brother/sister=2, uncle=3, grandparents=4); source of investment capital (formal=0, informal=1); nature of enterprise ownership (family=0), (sole personal=1, partnership=2, joint stock=3, cooperative society=4); and marital status (marriage=0, divorce=1, separated=2), (widow=3). Among these variables, all variables except experience and marital status significantly influenced the variation in investment decision which was very important for growth and level of income of an economy.

Though there were many macro-economic policy variables, Barro (2013) focused on human capital as a determinant of economic growth. Among the components of human capital (education, health and aspects of social capital), he emphasised on education. His study examined the factors that determined economic growth and investment in a panel of around 100 countries observed from 1960-1995.

Conditional convergence was found in the sense that the relation between growth rate of per capita GDP and starting (initial) level of per capita GDP was inverse one, keeping other variables held constant.

The growth rate was positively related to starting level of average years of attainment of adult males at the secondary and higher levels. This complementary relation indicated the important role of education for diffusion of technology in the process of economic growth. This relation was not found in the case of female. This suggested that highly educated women workers were not utilised in the labour market in many countries. Unlike male, education of women at primary level stimulates growth indirectly through lower fertility rate. Among the proxies (cross country comparable examination in science, mathematics and reading) to measure the quality of schooling, score on science test had strong positive relation with economic growth rate.

Recognizing the importance of education as one of the primary components of human capital in new growth theories or endogenous growth theories, Pegkas (2014) attempted to examine the relationship between the levels of education and economic growth to estimate the effects of each level of education on economic growth in Greece during the period of 1960-2009. The study employed the Mankiw, Romer and Weil (1992) model and VAR analysis. The enrolment rates were used as proxy for human capital. His finding revealed that there was a long run relationship between educational levels and gross domestic product. The overall results revealed that secondary and higher education had a statistically significant positive impact on growth while primary education had not much significant influence on growth in the short run. However the importance of primary education could not be negated as primary was the first level of education of higher levels of education. Further, he concluded that primary education was more growth enhancing factor in less developed countries, while growth in developed countries was more influenced by higher and secondary education.

Maubrigades (2015) attempted to examine the relationship between women age at marriage and social and long term economic development in eight Latin American countries. Three temperate climate economies (Argentina, Uruguay and Chile) and other two groups that depend on size: the large and the middle size economies on the one hand (Columbia and Mexico) and the smaller economies (Ecuador, Guatemala and Panama) on the other. The period of study covered from 1930 to 2000. Like other studies she treated age at marriage as a measure of women bargaining power and an indicator of degree of freedom. Her finding suggested that there were three distinct marriage patterns in the region. First, in the southern cone countries, the marriage pattern was closest to that of the modern Western Europe. In this region, age at first marriage was higher and these countries experienced structural social changes and increase in educational attainment, urbanisation and the participation of women in the process of economic growth. Colombia and Mexico (group of large countries) have culturally and ethnically more diverse and women of these countries experienced younger marriage pattern than in the first group "even though women's years of study were gradually increasing and economic growth should offer more labour opportunities for them". The third group consisting Ecuador, Guatemala and Panama in which majority people were indigenous whose marriage pattern were farther from the European model. In these countries, economic growth was below the average of her panel countries and education of women improved very slowly. Sarker et al. (2016) attempted to identify the casual relationship between urban population and economic growth in South Asia using a panel data. To obtain the above objective, the study employed Augmented Dickey-Fuller (ADF) and Phillips Perron (PP), Pessaran as well as Fisher methods for panel unit root test. Their study found that in short run, there was no relation between urban population and economic growth in South Asia. Therefore, this relation implied that urban population growth did not immediately effect on economic growth in South Asia. But in the long run, the study concluded that there was significant impact on economic growth in the region.

2.2 Agricultural Production and Socio-Economic Variables

Chadha (2003) in his presidential address published in Indian Journal of Agricultural Economics, pick up three specific issues for Indian Agriculture in the New Millennium. Education for technological challenges is one of them. He gave various reasons for the important role of education to be played in tomorrow. With the changing farm inputs, commercial information and transport and communication, farmers' choices and chance of erring are also plentiful. The role of education has been paramount for creating proper knowledge and skill to learn these changes. Moreover, the relevance of education has also paramount importance for bridging rural and urban gap and male and female differences and for strengthening the grassroots democratic institutions. Numerous soil-related and environmental issues were highly correlated with sustainability of agriculture and occupational safety of the agriculturalist. These issues are to be solved through education. Diversifications of agriculture have good bearing on the increase of income. This could be created through adjustment in cropping pattern, mounting of allied agro-activities and shifts of occupation. These activities have required a high degree of awareness, market influence and alertness, quality consciousness and price competitiveness. These prerequisites could be achieved through proper education. In the environment of increasing commercialisation of agriculture, every farmer was required not only an efficient producer but also well informed market strategist. All these could be achieved through education and training.

Ramasamy et al. (1992) attempted to examine variables influencing on the adoption rates of modern varieties and explored their effects on fertiliser use and rice cropping intensity as well as on the adoption of labour saving technologies across different rice production environments. To achieve the above objectives, stratified random sampling was used covering 50 villages representing five different rice production environments in Tamil Nadu. The five production environments were rain fed-tank irrigated, tank irrigated, tank-well irrigated, river-canal irrigated, and reservoir-canal irrigated rice areas. For estimating the regression parameters they used two-limit profit regression method. The variables included were irrigation intensity, regional dummies for five environments, farm size, literacy, paddy price, area under share cropping, market distance, input prices (tractor rent, thresher rent and bullock wage), and production risk. Their findings for cross-sectional difference in adoption of modern varieties, fertiliser use, yield and rice cropping intensity were mainly explained by environmental rather than socio-economic factors.

While Rao (2003) examined the levels of technical efficiency in the production of rice, groundnut and cotton in Andhra Pradesh, he also attempted to identify the factors associated with technical efficiency. Improvement in technical efficiency has been a major source of production growth. To obtain the above objectives stochastic frontier production with a composed error term was used and farm level data were collected for these crops from West Godavari, Anantapur and Prakasam. In the case of rice production, the changes in technical efficiency levels were significantly determined by age and education of farmers and the proportion of area under rice to the total cropped area. Higher age, considered as a proxy for experience and education of farmer improved the technical efficiency. Education helped in better crop management decisions as well as placed the farmers in receiving right and proper information and extension services. Higher proportion of area under the crop enabled farmers to provide higher time and attention to the crop. Education, proportion of area under this crop to the total cropped area and farm size were factors which significantly influenced technical efficiency in groundnut production. Similarly, all the above variables that is age, education, percent area under this crop and farm size were found to have significantly influenced on technical efficiency in cotton production.

Randhir and Krishnamoorthy (1990) revealed that the variations of productivity in terms of income among the tank fed areas and the influence of resources used on these variations. For this a purposive sampling was conducted in Changalpattu district of Tamil Nadu during 1987-88. Logarithmic transformation of Cobb-Douglas production function was used and applied OLS method for estimation. The variables included in their study were total value of crop output of the farm (in rupees per net hectare), cropping intensity (in percentage), managerial skill index, labour used (in man hours per net hectare), amount of capital (in rupees per net hectare) average quality of water (in cm. per net hectare) and dummy variables for irrigation and tenancy status. They defined the managerial skill index as

$$S = \frac{Mi}{M} \times 100$$

where, $Mi = 1M_1 + 2M_2 + 3M_3$

M_1 = number of years of schooling,

M_2 = years of experiences in farming

M_3 = farm training undergone if any

M = mean of Mi

The results of the study have clearly shown that there was a productivity variation among different farm sizes even under homogeneous irrigation situations. This shows potential productivity of marginal farms through community wells. The cropping intensity most significantly influenced on the farm income. This was followed by labour and capital. Interestingly it was also indicated that the managerial skill coefficient was not significant even at 10% level of significance.

Roy and Pal (2002) examined determinants of agricultural

productivity in Indian states while they tried to explain poverty, analysis of the growth in agriculture as well as its determinant by using data from All India Debt and Investment survey by RBI and National Sample Organisation and Finance Accounts of the Centre and States. By employing 2 Stage Least Square Method for simultaneous equation they concluded that per hectare agricultural state domestic product was significantly influenced by all variables included in the simultaneous equation except road density per hectare. The significant variables were rural literacy rate, population growth rate, percentage of population below poverty line, per hectare public investment, per hectare private agricultural investment, population growth rate, percent area under marginal holdings, subsidy, terms of trade, institutional credit to agriculture, cropping intensity, storage capacity and rainfall index.

Tripathy et al. (2006) while studying on the trend of production, adoption and utilisation of high quality paddy seeds, they attempted (in one of the sections) to identify the contribution of various factors to the adoption and utilisation of high quality seeds which were very closely connected to agricultural productivity. Data were collected by using multi-stage random sampling method from 30 districts of Orissa. For estimating the coefficients of variables Logit Model was employed. The variables included in the model may be enumerated as age and number of years spent in educational institutions, land holding of the farmers, price of factor inputs and distance from seeds sale centres and dummy variables for regions of Orissa. The probability of adoption and utilisation of rice seeds in Orissa was inversely related with the age of farmers, input prices and the distance from the seeds sale centre but was directly related to the number of years schooling, land holding size and the regional location of the farmers' households.

Soil and water conservations are very important for production and productivity in the riverine belt. In this context, Barman and Das (2010) examined the impact of socio-economic and institutional factors on the adoption of various soil and water conservation practices in the riverine belt of Assam - riverine areas of Lakhimpur and Sonitpur districts of Assam. Data were collected randomly in the year 2007-08. A Tobit model was used to achieve the above objective using the following independent variables of social variables (age, educational level and family size), diffusion variables (awareness, perception), physical variables (soil, slope, soil characteristics and farm fragmentation), economic variables (income, farm size, off farm employment) and institutional variable (land tenure). Among these variables, family size (proxy for availability of farm labour), awareness (for informal education, training and awareness programmes), perception (of effects of soil and water degradation on crop yield, and of profitability of conservation techniques), number of days spent on off farm employment and land tenure were significant variables influencing soil and water conservation practices.

Rice-wheat productivity data showed an increasing trend for the period of 1960-2000, then afterwards if became a decreasing or stagnating (Kumar et al., 2010). This latter trend could be attributed to improper intensive agricultural farming. To solve the problem intensive farming resulting to environmental problem which led to the whole system unsustainable, zero tillage technology could be used. Zero tillage was defined as planting of crops in "previously unprepared soil by opening narrow slots or trenches of the smallest width and depth needed for proper coverage of the seed". In this background, they attempted to examine the benefit of this technology and to identify the factors influencing its adoption in wheat crop for rice-wheat system on three different regions of Indo-Gangetic plains of Haryana, Bihar and Uttar Pradesh. The maximum likelihood estimates of Logit Model indicated negative and significant impact of age of farmers on the probability of technology adoption in these three states. The older farmers were adverse to the latest technology while young farmers had a larger risk taking ability. The sign of education was positive indicating the probability of technology adoption but the co-efficient was not significant in Haryana. However, the coefficient was negative and significant in the case of Uttar Pradesh and Bihar. This was explained by the fact that the involvement of educated generation had declined. The impact of farming experience was found to be positive and significant. Availability of credit was found to have significant and positive impact on adoption of zero tillage. Social interaction and implementation of government programmes, participation in village community meeting, expose to mass media, participation in farmers' fairs and visit of extension officers were found to have varying result in these three States.

D'Souza et al. (1993) attempted to determine the characteristics associated with the adoption of sustainable decision and revealed policy implications of them. To achieve these objectives a Logit Model was applied to the data from 1990 survey of West Virginia farmers. They defined sustainable agriculture as a system of agricultural activities involving the use of combination of appropriate practices or technologies selected from among the following: (a) manure, crop rotation, integrated pest management, rotational grazing, tillage for seed bed preparation and cultivation for weed control and simultaneously (b) reduction in the use of petroleum base products, chemical fertilisers, pesticides, hormones and antibodies. The study has shown that the adoption of sustainable is significantly determined by human capital characteristics such as a producer's age and education. Unlike the findings of other studies on technology adoption, the coefficients for structural and institutional characteristics (except for off farmer employment) such as farm size, debt/ asset ratio and hired labour are not significant. They confirmed their hypotheses – an environmental characteristic and ground water quality have a significant impact on the adoption of sustainable production system.

Anigbogu et al. (2015) examined socio-economic factors influencing agricultural production among cooperative farmers in Anambra state, Nigeria. Multi-stage sampling technique was used to obtain the data. Fourteen socio-economic variables – gender, age, marital status, educational qualification, farming experience, farm size, household size, income, credit obtain, seedling obtain, fertiliser obtain, type of technology, fertility of land and type of crop cultivated were taken into account for the analysis. Among these variables, 5 variables were used as dummy variables – Gender (1 for male, 2 for female), Marital status (1 for married, 0 for otherwise), type of technology (1 for capital intensive, 0 for otherwise), soil fertility (1 for fertile, 0 for otherwise) and crop type (1 for cash crop, 0 for otherwise). Out of the fourteen variables, seven variables – age, educational qualification, farming experience, income, seeding obtain, fertiliser obtain and fertility of the land – positively and significantly influenced the output of the farmers in 2011. Their findings were robust with varying insightful significance.

Obasi et al. (2013) investigated to find out the socio-economic factors that affect agricultural productivity in Imo State, Nigeria. The method of proportionate random sampling technique was used in selecting sampling units. Ordinary least square multiple regression analysis were used for analysing the collected data. Four functions viz. Linear, Double Log, Exponential and semi-log were fitted to the data. To make comparable the dependent variable, linear and semi-log function with double-log and exponential, the linear and semi-log dependent were transformed as

$$y^* = CY_t$$

where, Y_t^* = transformed dependent variable.
C = reciprocal of the geometric mean of Y values.
Y = original values of Y and period t.

Based on the value of R^2 and signs and size of the parameter estimated as well as statistical significance, the double log function was chosen as the lead equation and used for further analysis. Their findings revealed that educational level, farming experience, farm size, extension and labour had positive and significant relation with productivity. This implies that if these factors are increased above their present levels of use, productivity will increase. Increase in productivity is also expected if more educated and more experience farmers cultivate greater farm land. On the other hand, age, planting materials and chemical fertiliser were inversely related to productivity. This result suggests that productivity will decline if more of these factors are used above their present levels. Household size had negative sign but insignificant. This indicates that, productivity leads to decrease as it creates more cost rather than the value of output.

To find out the relationships between the socio-economic and paddy productivity, Alam et al. (2011) collected data through a sample survey. The survey with a structural questionnaire was conducted in North West Selangor, Malaysia. The data was analysed with OLS regressions. To solve the problem of heteroscedasticity, additional regression was conducted by the "White Heteroscedasticity Consistent Standard Errors and Covariance method with the help of Eviews econometric software". They considered 23 socio-economic variables. Among them, variables of secondary education, primary education, race and two locality variables were found significant. In addition to these variables farm size, number of machineries and ratio of non-agriculture to agricultural income significantly influenced productivity of paddy. Thus, they concluded that several socio-economic and physical characteristics had significant impact on paddy productivity in Malaysia.

2.3 Fertility and Socio-Economic Variables

Becker (1960) perhaps used general economic framework for the first time to analyze the determinants of fertility. Children were primarily treated as a consumers' durable commodity. Determinants of fertility considered by him in his analysis were income, child costs, knowledge of contraceptives, uncertainty and tastes. Among these variables he emphasized income. Like other consumer commodities, demand for children would increase when there has an increase in income and a decline in price or cost of children, since children are not inferior commodity. Increase in income would increase both quantity and quality (measured by amount spent on children) of children, but quantity elasticity was very small as compared to quality elasticity. He logically argued that the secular decline in fertility was inconsistent with this positive relation since contraceptive knowledge and child costs could easily offset the secular rise in income.

For the first time Easterlin (1969) attempted to build a socio-economic theory of fertility. In economic theory of fertility (of Becker) household choice on fertility was evaluated on the basis of the interaction between preferences on one hand and income and price constraints on the other. Thus, income, prices and taste were three building blocks for the household behaviour. Economists conceived nature of taste (that is, preference map) only embracing all possible combinations of goods. A household's desire for any commodity including children must be evaluated in the context of attitude towards other goods. They disliked the details of formation of taste which were emphasized by sociologists. He argued one's preference was molded by heredity and past and current environment. In shaping of tastes, religion, colour, nativity, place of residence, age, education etc. played the major role. Thus, for a complete and meaningful theoretical framework for fertility, Easterlin emphasized the integration of socio-economic factors and understanding the relevance of each others' (economist and sociologist) contributions. Recognizing the perverse relationship (in terms of magnitude and direction) between socio-economic factors and fertility, Bongaarts (1978) attempted another approach to explain the variation in fertility through proximate determinants (intermediate variables). He defined proximate determinants as the biological and behavioral factors through which socio-economic, cultural and environmental variables affected fertility. If an intermediate variable changed, the fertility was also changed, other things remained the same. Broadly there have been eight intermediate factors – proportion married, contraception, induced abortion, lactation, infecundability, frequency of intercourse, sterility, spontaneous intrauterine mortality and duration of fertility period. The finding of his investigation indicated that marriage, contraception, lactation and induced abortion were the primary proximate determinants of fertility variations among the population. The model could be valuable in the analysis of socio-economic determinants of fertility because these proximate variables allowed the identification of the way through which various socio-economic variables affected fertility.

Borg (1989) studied to explain the inconsistency between the hypotheses and empirical findings of many studies about the relationship between fertility and income. His finding revealed that the positive relationship hypothesis of income and fertility could be proved clearly when proxy variables for the net price of a child were included in empirical fertility models. If net price variables – the opportunity cost, the wife's time in child rearing and other costs and benefits of children were eliminated from the estimated model, the income coefficient became negative and significant rather than positive and significant. Therefore, it was argued strongly that net price of children variables should be given high priority in fertility surveys. Rob (1992) investigated the relationship between fertility, on one hand and factors which were often examined in many studies – education, employment, land ownership, family income and religion, on the other. Empirical findings suggested that the relation between socio-economic variables and fertility were not always consistent, particularly in developing countries. He warned future researchers to take care in explaining the influence of socio-economic variables on fertility.

Murthi et al. (1995) found that since population growth in India was often of intense concern, it was worth reiteration that the only variables we found to have a significant effect on fertility were female literacy and female labour force participation. Besides, there was likely to be a significant causal link between mortality and fertility with the latter going down as mortality declines. The direct promotion of child health, female literacy and female labour force participation was likely to be more conducive to lowering fertility than indirect interventions based on promoting economic development.

Unlike other studies, Sidhiqui (1996) studied on international comparison of fertility behaviour based on two crucial assumptions. Firstly, the relation between fertility rates and socio-economic factors was similar across different age cohorts of female population in the reproductive age group and secondly, country specific effects did not influence the parameter estimates of the fertility model. Recent availability of cross-country data for a number of years allowed to pool data for more than 100 years for the period of 1955-1985 and estimate the fertility model. It was observed that the impact of socio-economic factors differed across different age-cohorts, particularly the negative impact of empowerment in female status on the fertility rates was higher among the young age-cohorts. Also the cross-country differences affect fertility rates significantly. The differences tended to diminish as countries become more developed. These indicated that not only cross-country differences but also the changes in age composition of female population should be taken into account in formulating the policies to control fertility and population growth. Improvement in female literacy shall be most important.

Dre`ze and Murthi (1999) attempted to find out the factors which were important for changes in fertility in India by using a multivariate framework with district level panel data of 1981 and 1991. One of the most striking findings was extremely robust relationship between female literacy and fertility in India. The impact of female literacy was negative and highly significant in determining fertility. Moreover, low level of child mortality and son preference had significant impact on the variation in fertility. But, their finding suggested that there was tenuous relation between fertility decline and male literacy, urbanization and poverty. Savitri (1994) also reported another interesting finding on the determinants of variation in fertility among the inter-districts of Tamil Nadu in different periods. Analysis of inter-district variation in fertility revealed that availability of road facilities and child mortality were the major determinants. Better road increased the rural-urban connectivity. In rural area the fertility behaviour depended on consumer price (of food grains) and index of agricultural labour. In other words there was a strong impact of poverty along with better rural-urban linkages on the fertility behaviour in Tamil Nadu. Unlike other studies, her finding suggested that poor families (rural families) had lower fertility because better rural-urban connectivity enabled rural people to take the urban facilities including urban jobs, urban education for their children without shifting their residence to urban areas. Moreover, they believed that they could get a better way of life and could cope better the increasing price situation by reducing their family size.

James (1999) attempted to explain the causal factors responsible for the dramatic fertility decline in Andhra Pradesh. Unlike other Southern States like Kerala where replacement level of fertility has already been attained, the influences of female literacy level and health status of the people on fertility were weak in this state. The decline was mainly due to the striking changes of rural economy particularly during 1980's. Among the changes the notables were vigorous public distribution system through which 80% of people received rice at a very low price, improvement of standard of living attained through pumping of large amount of money through various schemes. As a result of these measures population below poverty line declined dramatically. The decline in fertility was associated with the decline in unemployment and rise in the wage rate particularly in rural areas. He argued that improvement of this labour market had the implication of decline in the role of children as economic security. Moreover, he noted paradoxically variables like literacy of mother or father appeared not to explain contraceptive use. Roy et al. (1999) tried to explore economic rationality of fertility preference in Punjab, Maharashtra, Kerala and Uttar Pradesh by using data of National Family Health Survey (NFHS) 1995. Negative association between economic status (standard of living) and fertility change was found in Punjab. Such negative relation was also found in other remaining three states though to a lesser extent and it was more evident in higher educated group. Strong negative relation between fertility and size of land holding was seen only in Punjab. It is worth to mention that there was no impact of standard of living on the attitudes of couples towards ideal family size in Kerala. They argued that the relationship between standard of living and economic condition with fertility had remained at best unclear and a set of social factors directly influenced couple'sdecision on family size.

Using a sample of 106 countries, Ghannam (2005) highlighted that among the less developed countries (LDC) the fertility rate was at least triple as high as among the More Developed Countries (MDC). Data were collected from various sources including United Nations Statistical Yearbook 2002, World's Woman Trends and Statistics, Social Indicators of Development published by UNO 2000. These countries were divided by region of the world – 21 from East and South Africa, 17 from West Africa, 10 from East Asia and Pacific, 6 from South Asia, 11 from Eastern Europe and Central Asia, 20 from Europe, 4 from Middle East, 3 from North America and 14 from Latin America. He investigated the relationship between fertility rate differentials and child mortality, female life expectancy, age at the first marriage for women, mean years of women education, and participation of woman in labour force among the LDC and MDC countries. The study also attempted to determine empirically which of these factors were more significant in affecting fertility rate differentials. The interpretation of data was based on the demographic transition theory. According to World Bank report (1999), 53 of these countries were considered as LDCs, low income group, while others 53 were treated as MDCs, high income group. The findings of the descriptive analysis revealed that the mean total fertility rate for LDCs was 6.1, while the mean in MDCs was 2.1. It suggested that increase total fertility rate in LDCs occurred significantly among women who were having more children died, more number of years of life expectancy, more participation in labour force. In addition to this, the result indicates that total fertility rate decreased among women in MDCs who have more number of years of female life expectancy and more participation in labour force. The fertility among LDCs was at least triple as high as among the MDCs Method.

The study of Khan and Khan (2010) was to find out demand side determining the factors of contraceptive use by married women in Pakistan. Their approach was also a kind of finding out fertility determining factor assuming the close relationship between the use of contraceptive and the level of fertility. Probit model was used in analyzing the primary data collected from the reproductive age group (15-49 years) of two districts in Pakistan. The majority of factors under study were intertwined and mutually reinforcing, which have contributed to low contraceptive use. Predominance of male was shown. The household income, husband education, husband's age at marriage, number of living children, number of sons, household income and urban characteristics of household significantly influenced the use of contraceptive among women. Chani et al. (2012) conducted an empirical study to investigate the role of various socio-economic factors like female education, urbanization and female labour force participation in determining fertility of women in Pakistan covering a period from 1980 to 2009. Utilizing regression model, they observed that urbanization played a major role in controlling fertility because in urban areas rearing of child is costly; and secondly, educated women had less fertility than illiterate females. But female work force participation remained insignificant in reducing fertility. This might be due to lack of the opportunity of female participation in work force in Pakistan.

Using the National Demographic and Health Survey

(NDHS) 2008 data collected by National Statistical Office, Siow-Li Lai (2014) analysed the socio-conomic and proximate determinants of fertility in Philippines. Bongaarts Model was used to estimate the indices of the four main proximate determinants of fertility. The findings highlighted that fertility differentials were affected by ethnic group, place of residence, educational attainment, women's work and family wealth. These socio-economic factors influence fertility mainly through the composition of age, age at marriage, contraceptive uses were important factors affecting fertility. It was also found that women from the poor background had children twice as much as that of the rich. The findings added that the population growth in Philippines was the highest among the South East Asia due to its high level of fertility. Adhikari (2010) found that traditionally Nepalese society favoured high fertility. For them children were symbol of well-being both socially and economically. Even if fertility was decreasing in Nepal since 1981, it was still high as compared to many other developing countries. Using the data from the Nepal Demographic and Health Survey (NDHS-2006) of 8644 married women of reproductive age, he performed the analysis with both bivariate and multivariate analysis to study the fertility differentials. It was found that there were many contributing factors for the high fertility among which the important ones were age at first marriage, perceived ideal number of children, literacy status, mass media exposure, wealth status, and child deaths experience of mothers. All of these factors were strong predictors for CEB. The study concluded that programme should aim to reduce fertility rates by focusing on these identified factors so that fertility as well as infant and maternal mortality and morbidity be decreased and the overall well-being of the family maintained and enhanced.

Dribe (2014) studied the relationship between socio-economic status and fertility during and after the demographic transition using micro level econo-demographic data for five communities/areas in Sweden, Netherlands, Italy, United States and Canada covering the period from early 19th century until the mid-20th century. More specifically, he looks at the development of socio-economic differences in marital fertility and relates it to common theories of fertility behaviour as adjustment and innovated process. Their finding did not support the hypothesis of universally high fertility among the upper classes in pre-transitional society rather it supported the idea that they were forerunners in reducing fertility. Farmers and unskilled labour were found followers in reducing fertility. Kreyenfeld and Andersson (2014) surveyed a large body of research on the economic determinants of child bearing behaviour. They found that most of the empirical works assumed that economic hardship and labour market uncertainties would cause people to postpone their fertility plans. In this study, they examined how the association of unemployment and fertility varied with socio subgroups using data from the German Socio-Economic Panel (GSOEP) and from Danish Population Registers. They found that male unemployment was related to a postponement of first and second childbearings in both countries while the role of female unemployment was found less clear. Both male and female unemployment were positively correlated with third birth. More importantly, the results pointed out that there was strong correlation between fertility and educational unemployment in various socio-economic groups. Fertility tended to be lower during periods of unemployment among highly educated women and men but not among their less educated counter-parts.

In the history of fertility transition, Martin et al. (2014) highlighted that there was still a lack of knowledge about disaggregated patterns that could help to understand the mechanisms behind the transition. In view of this they attempted to study socio-economic pattern in the fertility transition in different situations using similar approaches and measures of socio-economic status. Using different kinds of micro level socio-economic and demographic data collected within from census-records or population registers in Sweden during 1880-1970 the study showed there was no consistent evidence for the hypothesis that socio-economic status was positively related to fertility before the demographic transitions. In the study, correlation was clearly present in some contexts while it was clearly not in others. It was also found that the upper and middle experienced the forerunners in transition while farmers had slower change in their fertility behaviour.

Breschi et al. (2014) attempted to demonstrate the importance of social and economic factors in determining natural fertility before the diffusion of contraceptives. In order to find out the importance of non-biological components, the study focuses six pre transitional communities situated in different parts of Italy. In order to estimate the impact of socio-economic factors on fertility, micro-level data were collected from different historical sources and discrete time event history models were applied to female reproductive behaviours. Their finding showed that before fertility decline the main determinant of fertility was biological and physiological factors and socio-economic factors played minor role in regulating the fertility. Yurtseven (2015) attempted to find out the determinants of fertility in predominantly Muslim countries. These countries had higher fertility rates on average than those of Western Countries. A sample of 33 predominantly Muslim countries was taken to obtain the above objective. Lots of explanatory variables were utilized such as income per capita income, education, labour force participation, unemployment, pre-primary school, enrolment, college enrolment, contraceptive prevalence, gender inequality, first age at marriage and marriage rate as the determinants of fertility rate. His finding indicated that the past realization of fertility, income, college enrolment rate, contraceptive and time trend were the significant determinants of fertility. These findings were in line with the results of the studies that found in non-Muslim and mainly western countries. All the signs of the explanatory variables were in line with the theory. It was also found that in general, countries in the study have higher gender inequality, unemployment rates, marriage rates and lower education levels, college enrolment and first age at marriage all of which contributed to higher fertility rates. The variation in these socio-economic variables would invariably cause a decline in fertility rates in the coming years.

Mohanty et al. (2015) attempted to examine the relation between the change in fertility and female literacy, under-five mortality and poverty by using census and large-scale population surveys over the last two decades (1991-2011). The study covered the evidence from 610 Indian districts. Their paper revealed that there was significant degree of convergence across all determinants under study but only limited convergence for fertility was found. The result of their study found that the strong relation between the level and changes of female literacy with the variation in fertility. Such relation was also shown in the case of fertility and under-five mortality, despite to a lesser degree while the impact of improved socio-economic status was negligible. Chandiok et al. (2016) attempted to find out biological and social determinants of fertility among the Jat women of Haryana by surveying households in 15 villages of Palwal district. They found that age at marriage, educational status, family type and son preference were the main factors that have significant influence on the variation in fertility. The study reported that age at menarche, age at first conception, occupational status, use of birth control measures and household per capita income did not affect the variation in fertility. Moreover, their work manifested the importance of community specific study for community population planning.

Awad et al. (2017) also studied to investigate the main determinants of total fertility rates in Malaysia during the period between 1980 and 2014 by using Autoregressive Distributed Lag method. Their findings revealed that in the long run, GDP, females' education and employment influenced total fertility negatively and significantly. But during the short period only infant mortality was significant and positive. The overall findings of this study indicate that demographic and socio-economic variable were major determinant for declining trend in total fertility in Malaysia. Alemayehu (2017) assessed socio-economic factors that deterred the growth of fertility in Hosanna town, South Ethiopia. Multi stage and simple random sampling techniques were employed for collecting data. The collected data were analysed with the help of descriptive statistics. The study revealed relation between the fertility and the first age at marriage, educational level, birth space and income level of women and birth space between two consecutive children. Moreover, occupational factors and religion of a woman were significant factors for determining fertility. Muslim women experienced high fertility while Catholic respondents had relative low fertility. Regarding occupation type, housewife respondents, self-employed women and currently employed women had highest, medium and low fertility respectively.

On the whole, what can be drawn from the above review is that socio-economic factors significantly determine the variation in income, agricultural production and human fertility in different parts of the world. The significance was tested through various methods of estimations. Different socio-economic variables were taken into account. The degree of influence varied from place to place and method to method. Moreover, few studies were made in underdeveloped hilly areas in general and north-east states in particular. The following chapters will considered this issue. Moreover, in view of the above backdrop a study on the impact of socio-economic factors on income, rice production and human fertility would help much in implementing socio-economic policy in hill areas on priority basis.

3

Chapter

Profile of Chandel District

3.1 General Characteristics

Till 1969 Manipur was under a single district having 10 sub-divisions. Chandel was one of them. As per district reorganization in 1969, the entire state was divided into 5 districts and the former sub-divisions further sub-divided into 25 sub-divisions. The present Chandel district was a sub-division under the name of Tengnoupal sub-division. In 1974 Tengnoupal district was carved out of the erstwhile Manipur Central District under Manipur Gazette Extra-Ordinary No. 30, dated 11th May, 1974 having three sub-divisions namely Chandel (687 sq.km.), Chakpikarong (1413 sq.km.) and Tengnoupal (775 sq.km.). As Chandel was the district Headquarters, Tengnoupal was christened into Chandel District under Extra-Ordinary Manipur Gazette Notification No.174 on 5th August, 1983. On 3rd January, 1994 another sub-division namely Machi (438 sq. km) was created. Now the district has 4 sub-divisions. In 2011 the total population of Chandel was 144,182 of which 74,579 were male and 69,603 were female. The population of Chandel comprised 5% of the total state population. Out of the total district population 89% was scheduled tribe, only 0.4% was scheduled caste and 10.6% was others. In this district, 88.32% of the population settled in rural area and the rest 11.68% settled in urban area. The district occupies a geographical area of 3,313 sq.km. that is 14.8% of the total state area. It is situated to the south part of the state and located between 23°45–24°45 North latitude and 94°48-94°30 East longitude. It is bounded by Ukhrul and Senapati in the north, south and south-east by Myanmar and by Thoubal and Churachandpur district in the west. The highest altitude in the district is 145.3 metre above sea level. Maximum temperature is 42.0 Celsius degree with a minimum temperature of 6.0 Celsius degree. The district is influenced by sub-tropical monsoon climate. The average relative humidity ranges from 22% to 100%. Winter starts from October and lasts till February while the summer starts from March and ends in July. It is moderately hot but Moreh a small town located on the international border with Myanmar is hotter than other area of the district. The district enjoys adequate rainfall which starts from March and continues up to September. The distribution of rainfall in the region and its neighbouring area is more or less uniform at the average of 2752 mm. The Chandel District is sparsely inhabited. Density of population is 44 per sq.km. in 2011 census. But this does not mean that the district has plenty of cultivable lands. There are many barren hill slopes and unproductive forest area. The 350 revenue villages spread in 4 sub-divisions and 9 urban wards within 1 sq.km in Moreh. The district has only two assembly constituencies viz. 41/AC (ST) Chandel, 42/AC (ST) Tengnoupal.

3.2 Topography

Chandel district comprises hill slope towards the east and west. A long range stretches in the middle of the district from north to south and it is as high as 2372 metre at Nangte Vum which divides the river system into two, thus one flowing towards eastward and falling into the Myanmar river and another falling into Manipur river. The district is divided into the three hilly regions namely Western, Eastern and Southern region. Major portions of Tengnoupal, Machi and Chandel are covered by western hill region. The important peaks are Eavoiching (1933 m), Sita Chingjao (1597 m), Mitong Khullen (1580 m) etc. The eastern hilly region in the north eastern corner of the district occupies Larong Khunou (1241 m), Doleiching (1193 m), Narum (1099 m), Sibong (839 m), Sita Hangching (745 m) etc. The entire Chakpikarong sub-division falls within the southern region with 7 peaks Nangte

Vum (2372m), Halbolching (2085 m), Lingpongching (1763 m), Khaichingbung (1707 m), Shaikui (1593 m), Khullen Khaillet (1561 m) and Aibol Joupi (1401 m). There are two main river ranges. The tributaries of Manipur river like Chakpi, Kohalok and Sekmai rivers drain the western portion while Taretlok, Lokchou, Tuidam, Tinaham, Tuisadung rivers drain the eastern portion of the district. None of these rivers is navigable but is economically useful for catching fish and drinking purposes.

3.3 People

The study population, Chandel district is inhabited by different ethnic communities of Aimol, Anal, Lamkang, Maring, Mao, Mizo (Lusai), Monsang, Moyon, Paite, Thadou, Vaiphei, Zou, Chothe, Tarao, Meitei, Muslim and other generic tribes. Among them, Anal, Maring, Thadou, Vaiphei and Zou form the Major tribes in the district. Anal tribe spreads in Chandel and Chakpikarong sub-divisions, while Maring in Machi sub-division and Thadou, Vaiphei and Zou inhabitate in all the three sub-divisions of Tengnoupal, Chandel and Chakpikarong. There is one scheduled caste village at Kwatha. A good number of non-locals also settle at Moreh for trade and commerce. These varied ethnic groups in the district have different implication to socio-economic development.

3.4 Population Growth

The decennial population growth rate in Manipur declined from 29.29% during 1981-91 to 24.50% during 2001-11 (Table-3.1). During the same decades the growth rate in Chandel district declined from 25.87% to 21.89%. The decline of decennial population growth may perhaps be due to the adoption of family welfare programme in the state. However, irregularities in the growth rate in the Chandel were observed during the period under observation. The sudden jump or so termed rapid growth rate during 1991-2001 that is 66.62% might perhaps be attributed mainly to immigration from across the border areas especially in Chakpikarong and Tengnoupal sub-divisions. The sub-division wise annual growth rate of population in the district shows that the highest growth rate was found in Chakpikarong (6.94%) and followed by Tengnoupal (4.04%) and Chandel (3.49%) respectively. Improvement in public health care might also have contributed to this rapid growth rate in one sense which might again link with low death rate despite negligible.

Table–3.1
Size of population in Manipur and Chandel District

State /District	Year Wise Population ('00)		
	1991	2001	2011
Manipur	18,372 (29.29)	22,939 (24.86)	28,558 (24.50)
Chandel	710 (25.87)	1.183 (66.62)	1,442 (21.89)

Figures in parenthesis indicate decadal growth rate (in %)
Sources: Economic Survey Manipur 2013-2014 (Directorate of Economics & Statistics, Govt. of Manipur)

3.5 Population Density

One of the important features of population density is that the average density of population in the five hill districts was about 1/11 of the average density of population in four valley districts in 2011. The Chandel District which is one of the five hill districts is sparsely populated as its density of population was 44 per sq.km. (Table–3.2). Though the density was very low as compared to valley districts and Manipur (128), the density in the district was the middle (44) among the hill districts, the lowest being in Tamenglong (32) while the highest was found in Senapati (146). It may also be noted that during the seven censuses (1951-2011) the density increased very slowly from 7(1951) to 12(1981) then it increased with a sudden step that is 21 in 1991 which further increased to 36 in 2001 and to 44 in 2011. This sudden increase might be due to immigration and improving socio-economic factors including health, transport and communication etc. The sub-division wise population density in 2011 revealed that it was 51 in Tengnoupal having an area of 775 sq.km.;

37 in Chakpikarong (1413 sq.km.); 47 in Chandel (687 sq.km.) and 45 in Machi (438 sq.km.).

Table–3.2

District wise distribution of important socio demographic levels of Manipur according to 2011 census

District	Population (% in total)	Decennial growth (%)	Percent to total Population		Population density (per sq.km.)	Sex ratio	Literacy rate (rank)
			ST	SC			
Imphal East	16.0	15.50	6.06	3.47	643	1017	81.95(3)
Imphal West	18.1	16.56	4.66	3.19	998	1031	86.08(1)
Bishnupur	8.3	13.93	1.38	9.31	479	999	75.85(5)
Thoubal	14.8	15.96	0.43	9.62	821	1002	74.47(6)
Senapati	16.8	68.94	79.76	0.37	146	937	74.13(7)
Tamenglong	4.9	26.19	95.72	0.02	32	943	70.05(9)
Churachandpur	9.6	20.27	92.94	0.16	60	975	82.78(2)
Chandel	5.0	21.89	88.97	0.37	44	933	71.11(8)
Ukhrul	6.5	30.68	94.35	0.13	40	943	81.35(4)
State	**100.00**	**24.50**	**35.12**	**3.78**	**128**	**985**	**79.2%**

Source: Economic Survey Manipur 2013-2014 (Directorate of Economic & Statistics, Govt. of Manipur)

3.6 Sex Ratio

Sex ratio which is defined as number of females per 1000 of males is one of the determinants of women status. Such important determinant was the lowest in the district (933) among the hill districts of Manipur (Table–3.2). The ratio also declined from 981 in 2001 census to 933 in 2011 (Table–3.3). This implies that the status of women in the district has been deteriorating. When examining sub-division wise, in 2001 census the ratio was highest in Chandel (1017) sub-division followed by that in Chakpikarong (978). In the next census too, the highest ratio was found in Chandel sub-division and followed by that in Machi (980). The ratio declined in all sub-divisions except in Machi during these two censuses. This implies that the status of women was highest in Chandel sub-division in both censuses, though it declined during these two censuses. And the status improved considerably in Machi while it declined in other sub-divisions.

Table–3.3
Sub-division wise sex ratio for rural population of Chandel in 2001-2011

Name of sub-division	No. of females per 1000 male	
	2001	2011
Machi	958	980
Tengnoupal	971	936
Chandel	1017	993
Chakpikarong	978	880
Moreh town	964	943
Chandel District	981	933

3.7 Literacy Rate

The Chandel district is developing in education. There are three degree colleges – a full-fledged Government College, United College at district head quarter and two grant-in-aid colleges namely South East Manipur College at Komlathabi (Tengnoupal sub-division) and Moreh College at Moreh (Tengnoupal sub-division). There are seven higher secondary schools, twenty-one high schools and two hundred thirty five primary schools in the district. The district has also one Industrial Training Institute (ITI) and two District Institute of Education and Training (DIET) centres. Literacy rate in Chandel district increased from 34.23% in 1981 to 71.11% in 2011 (Table–3.4). In spite of it Chandel district was still characterised by second lowest literacy rate (71) in 2011census while the lowest rate was found in Temenglong (70.05) (Table–3.2). It is interesting to note that the literacy rate in the only urban town in the district, Moreh (50.73) was low as compared to that of Chandel District (71.11). Sub-division wise literacy rate shows that in 1981 census the highest literacy rate (45.60) was found in Chandel Sub-division which was followed by 30.44% in Tengnoupal. And again, among the sub-divisions the highest literacy was found in Chandel (77.85) in 2011 and followed by Chakpikarong (71.81) in the same census.

The female literacy rate in Chandel district increased from

25.16 in 1981 census to 63.96 in 2011 census (Table–3.4). This increase in the rate was lower than the rate of the increase in the state (Manipur) where the rate increased from 29.06 in 1981 to 73.17 in 2011. Among the sub-divisions, the female literacy was found highest in Chakpikarong (78.18) and followed by Chandel (72.05) in 2011. The lowest rate was found in the newly bifurcated sub-division, Machi. It may also be noted that the literacy rate as well as female literacy rate in Chandel district were very much lower than those of the state.

Table–3.4
Literacy rate of Chandel by sub-division during 1981-2011

Sub-division/ District/ State/ Moreh Town	1981	1991	2001	2011
Tengnoupal	30.44 (20.48)	36.93 (26.71)	56.00 (39.87)	70.51 (62.45)
Machi	NA (39.98)	NA (52.43)	39.60	59.65
Chakpikarong	29.54 (21.72)	41.78 (28.78)	47.91 (42.35)	71.81 (78.18)
Chandel	45.60 (36.48)	62.96 (51.64)	73.60 (45.58)	77.85 (72.05)
Chandel district	34.23 (25.16)	46.68 (34.55)	56.22 (42.31)	71.11 (63.96)
Manipur state	41.35 (29.06)	59.89 (26.71)	70.53 (42.51)	79.21 (73.17)
Moreh Town	40.86	48.31	50.73	71.47 (62.88)

Figures in parentheses indicate female literacy rate

3.8 Distribution of Population by Worker and Non-Worker

Distribution of population by workers and non-workers reveals that in 2011 census percentage of non-workers was lowest in Chandel (47.12) among the hill districts of Manipur

(Table–3.5). This implies that 52.88% of the population of Chandel district was worker which was the highest among the hill districts of the state. Percentage of male non-worker (42.86) also was the lowest among the hill districts and female non-worker was the second lowest (51.69), the lowest being 51.03 which was found in Tamenglong. These figures reveal that the percentages of worker both male and female were almost the highest among the hill districts. In other words, the people of Chandel District are very labourous.

In spite of their diligence, they could not get proper employment opportunities and hence, the percentage of main worker in the district was in middle position (37.28) among the five hill districts. The highest percentage of main worker was found in Tamenglong (39.80) and the lowest was found in Churachandpur (32.75). The main female worker was found second lowest (28.58) in the district, the lowest being found in Churachandpur (23.81). But, the percentage of main male worker was found highest in Chandel district (45.40) followed by Tamenglong (42.20) and Churachandpur (41.46) respectively. The above discussion clearly shows that the lower working condition of Chandel people is due to inferior working situation of female worker. This is clearly supported by the percentage of marginal female worker in Chandel which was the highest (19.73) and it was much higher than those of Manipur as a whole (14.55) and hill districts as whole (13.17).

3.9 Distribution of Main Workers by Industrial Categories

The distribution of main workers by industrial categories reveals that out of the total main female worker the percentage of female cultivator accounted for 70.35 which was the second lowest among the hill districts in Manipur in 2011 census but the percentage was above the percentage in the state (Table–3.6). The percentage of male cultivator in the district was the lowest (53.84) among the hill districts. These figures imply that though agriculture has been the main stay of people in thedistrict the condition of farmers is very weak as compared to the condition of farmers in other districts because cultivator has better working condition than that of agricultural labourer.

Table–3.6
Distribution of main workers by industrial categories in 2011

State & Districts	Cultivators		Agricultural Labourers		Manufac-turing, processing, servicing & repairing in household industries		Other services	
	Male	Female	Male	Female	Male	Female	Male	Female
Senapati	76.51	85.69	2.27	3.25	1.09	1.34	20.17	9.11
Tamenglong	69.95	82.70	1.49	2.27	1.29	2.36	27.27	12.71
Churach-andpur	56.07	63.19	3.49	5.80	1.74	4.37	38.70	26.62
Chandel	53.84	70.35	3.93	7.36	1.32	3.43	40.91	18.93
Ukhrul	60.46	77.38	2.14	2.95	1.41	2.24	35.99	18.03
Hill Total	66.00	78.60	2.64	3.84	1.31	2.33	30.09	15.25
Manipur	45.71	51.70	3.99	5.87	43.89	8.89	48.03	33.54

Source: Statistical Year Book of Manipur 2016 (Directorate of Economics and Statistics, Govt. of Manipur)

This inference is further supported by the percentages of female agricultural labourer (7.36) in Chandel District which was the highest among the female agricultural labourer in hill districts. Similarly, the percentage of male agricultural labourer (3.93) was also highest among the figures of hill districts. If we compare between the percentages of male and female agricultural labourers, the condition of male worker is better than that of female. It is also worth to mention that higher percentage of female worker depended on agriculture. Percentages of male main worker employed in the industrial category of manufacturing, processing, servicing and repairing in household industry were almost the same in all hill districts of Manipur. But, the percentage of main female worker in this industrial category was the second highest in Chandel (3.43), the highest being in Churachandpur (4.37). Similarly, the percentage of main female worker in other services was found second highest in Chandel (18.93) which was next to that of Churachandpur (26.62). In the case of main male worker in other services the percentage was highest in the district followed by Churachandpur (38.70) and Ukhrul (35.99) respectively. The distribution of workers (both male and female) was negligible in other sectors – (a) livestock, forestry, fishing, hunting, plantation, orchard, and allied activities; (b) mining and quarrying; (c) manufacturing, processing, servicing and repairing other than household industry; (d) construction; (e) trade and commerce and (f) transport, storage and communication.

3.10 Surveyed Data Exploration

3.10a Distribution of Family Size by Sub-Division

In this section, the information obtained from the respondents of the surveyed population has been explored in terms of family size, agricultural activities and educational parameters – literacy rate, educational level, type of institutions in which most of the children studying, means of travelling to schools, number of drop out children etc. In this exploration of surveyed data, some of health related factors were also included. The factors were sources of drinking water, type of toilet/latrine used, major means of cooking etc. Besides, the variation in the percentage of some important demographic factors – women's age at marriage, women's age at first delivery, number of live births ever born to a couple, child mortality were also manifested.

The primary information of some interested factors by sub-division wise has been manifested in Table–3.7 to Table–3.13. The 1071 surveyed households of the study population in Chandel District of Manipur were distributed in four sub-divisions namely Tengnoupal (282), Machi (164), Chandel (232), and Chakpikarong (393) (Table–3.7). These households have been classified into four categories according to the size of family members say, at most 2, 3-5, 6-8 and more than 8 members. In the population only 4.4% of total households had at most two family members. At the same time, the highest proportion of 47.4% of total households had 3-5 members followed by 40.4% of 6-8 family members and the rest, 7.8% had more than 8 family members. In Chandel sub-division, the highest proportion of 48% of surveyed households had their family size of 3-5 members followed by 42% of the households which had 6-8 members and only 2% of those households were observed in the family size of more than 8 members. The similar pattern of the family size was also been observed in two other sub-division, say Machi and Tengnoupal. However, the highest proportion of 45.7% of the surveyed households in Chakpikarong sub-division had 6-8 family members followed by 40.7% with 3-5 members and 12.3% of the households had more than eight members in the sub-division. When categorizing the total surveyed households according to the number of male family members, the highest proportion of 34.5% of the households had exactly 2 male members. It is followed by 25.5% with exactly 3 male members. In this distribution, 14.4% of the study population had at most one male family member. However, the lowest proportion of 9.2% of study population had at least 5 male members. The similar pattern of variation was observed in all sub-divisions. The same nature of the variation in family size in terms of female members was also noted (Table–3.7).

Table–3.7

Sub-division wise distribution of size of family members

Factor	Category	Sub-Division				Total
		Tengnoupal	Machi	Chandel	Chakpikarong	
No. of family member	At most 2	6 (2.2)	11 (7.0)	19 (8.0)	5 (1.2)	47 (4.4)
	3-5 (52.2)	147 (46.5)	76 (48.0)	111 (40.7)	160 (47.4)	508
	6-8 (37.7)	106 (39.4)	65 (42.0)	97 (45.7)	180 (40.4)	433
	8 + (8.0)	23 (7.0)	11 (2.0)	5 (12.3)	48 (7.8)	83

	Total (100)	282 (100)	164 (100)	232 (100)	393 (100)	1071
No. of male family member	At most 1	27 (9.4)	27 (16.2)	61 (26.0)	48 (12.3)	154 (14.4)
	2	118 (42.0)	55 (33.8)	65 (28.0)	107 (27.2)	369 (34.5)
	3	57 (20.3)	47 (28.9)	64 (28.0)	107 (27.2)	273 (25.5)
	4	55 (19.6)	20 (12.0)	33 (14.0)	78 (19.8)	174 (16.3)
	At least 5	25 (8.7)	15 (9.2)	9 (4.0)	53 (13.6)	99 (9.2)
	Total	282 (100)	164 (100)	232 (100)	393 (100)	1071 (100)
No. of female family member	At most 1	35 (12.3)	27 (16.2)	42 (18.0)	48 (12.3)	154 (14.4)
	2	118 (42.0)	52 (31.7)	51 (22.0)	112 (28.4)	357 (33.3)
	3	55 (19.6)	43 (26.1)	70 (30.0)	107 (27.2)	264 (24.6)
	4	35 (12.3)	25 (15.5)	50 (22.0)	73 (18.5)	169 (15.8)
	At least 5	39 (13.8)	17 (10.6)	19 (8.0)	53 (13.6)	127 (11.9)
	Total	**282 (100)**	**164 (100)**	**232 (100)**	**393 (100)**	**1071 (100)**

3.10b Distribution of Agricultural Parameters

The study population (Chandel) is agro-based hill district in Manipur. The socio-economic status and standard of living of the people of Chandel are based on agricultural products generated from both jhum and wet cultivations. The surveyed households were categorized into three classes according to the area of cultivable (in acre) viz. less than one acre, one to three acres and more than three acres. About 56.4% of the surveyed households had 1-3 acres of cultivable land followed by 27.4% which had at least 3 acre of cultivable land and the least proportion of 16.2% which had at most one acres of cultivable land (Table–3.8). This shows most households possess medium size holdings of land.

The similar pattern of variation in the cultivable land available was seen in all sub-divisions despite the percentage of households having less than one acre was very high (38.2). When compared the size of holdings of different sub-divisions, it was also noticed that the highest percentage of households (39.7) which had the highest size of holding was found in Machi sub-division while the highest percentage of households (38.2) which had the lowest size of holding was found in Chakpikarong sub-division. When the surveyed households classified by number of male and female family member engaged in agricultural activities, it was found that the percentage of households declined with the increase in the number of person engaged in agriculture activities. It implies that the majority of households were with smaller number of agricultural worker. Among the sub-divisions, Chakpikarong witnessed the highest percentage (9.9) of households engaged higher number of male agricultural worker. On the contrary, in Chandel sub-division no households engaged four or more male workers in agricultural activities. In the case of female agricultural worker the highest percentage (21.1) of households engaged highest number of female workers in Machi while no household engaged female worker more than three in Chandel sub-division.

Table–3.8
Sub-division wise distribution of agricultural parameters

Factor	Category	Sub-Division				Total
		Tengnoupal	Machi	Chandel	Chakpikarong	
Area of cultivable	<1	20 (7.0)	20 (12.3)	32 (13.8)	150 (38.2)	174 (16.2)
land (in acre)	1-3	203 (72.1)	79 (47.9)	152 (65.5)	185 (47.1)	604 (56.4)
	3+	59 (20.9)	65 (39.7)	48 (20.7)	58 (14.7)	293 (27.4)

	Total	282 (100)	164 (100)	232 (100)	393 (100)	1071 (100)
No. of male family member engaged in agriculture	At most 1	119 (42.0)	79 (47.9)	139 (60.0)	151 (38.4)	487 (45.5)
	2	129 (45.7)	63 (38.7)	84 (36.0)	150 (38.2)	435 (40.6)
	3	20 (7.2)	19 (11.3)	9 (4.0)	53 (13.6)	102 (9.5)
	At least 4	14 (5.1)	3 (2.1)	0 (0.0)	39 (9.9)	47 (4.4)
	Total	282 (100)	164 (100)	232 (100)	393 (100)	1071 (100)
No. of female family member engaged in agriculture	At most 1	113 (39.9)	73 (44.4)	116 (50.0)	204 (51.9)	482 (45.0)
	2	133 (47.1)	77 (47.2)	83 (40.0)	116 (29.6)	458 (42.8)
	3	26 (9.4)	10 (6.3)	23 (10.0)	39 (9.9)	91 (8.5)
	At least 4	10 (3.6)	4 (21.1)	0 (0.0)	34 (8.6)	39 (3.6)
	Total	282 (100)	164 (100)	232 (100)	393 (100)	1071 (100)

3.10c Distribution of Literate Family Member

Table–3.9 shows the distribution of households according to number of literates of the surveyed households. Here, the households were distributed according to the five categories of at most one, two, three, four and at least five literate family members. In this table the highest proportion of 34.3% of the households in the district had at most two male literate members in the family followed by 31.9% households which had at most one male literate member.

The lowest of 3.9% households had at least five male literate members. On the whole it was shown that number of households having lower number of male literates was very high. It was also indicated that illiteracy rate of households was highest in Machi and followed by that of Chandel. It also revealed that the proportion of the surveyed households was monotonically decreasing with the increase in the number of literate females in Chandel District as well as in all four sub-divisions. Like male, female illiteracy households were highest in Machi (48.6) and followed by that in Chandel (44.0).

Table–3.9
Sub-division wise distribution of literate family member

Factor	Category	Sub-Division Tengn-oupal	Machi	Chandel	Chakpi-karong	Total
No. of male literate family member	At most 1	76 (26.8)	62 (38.0)	79 (34.1)	112 (28.4)	341 (31.9)
	2	108 (38.4)	53 (32.4)	78 (33.6)	121 (30.9)	367 (34.3)
	3	55 (19.6)	35 (21.1)	56 (24.1)	97 (24.7)	232 (21.7)
	4	25 (8.7)	10 (6.3)	14 (6.0)	48 (12.3)	89 (8.3)
	At least 5	18 (6.5)	4 (2.1)	5 (2.0)	15 (3.7)	42 (3.9)
	Total	282 (100)	164 (100)	232 (100)	393 (100)	1071 (100)
No. of female literate family member	At most 1	116 (41.3)	80 (48.6)	102 (44.0)	151 (38.3)	467 (43.6)
	2	92 (32.6)	47 (28.9)	56 (24.8)	212 (30.9)	320 (29.9)
	3	43 (15.2)	27 (16.2)	37 (16.0)	68 (17.3)	172 (16.1)
	4	27 (9.4)	5 (2.8)	37 (16.0)	34 (8.6)	83 (7.8)
	At least 5	4 (1.4)	6 (3.5)	0 (0.0)	19 (4.9)	29 (2.7)
	Total	282 (100)	164 (100)	232 (100)	393 (100)	1071 (100)

3.10d Distribution of Educational Level of Couple

The surveyed households was again categorized according

to the five educational levels of the couple – illiterate, literate but under matriculate, matriculate but below 10+2 standard, 10+2 but under graduate and at least graduate (Table–3.10). While classifying the population with the educational level of male spouse, nearly half (49.8%) of the households were observed in the families with literate but under matriculate. Only 11.7% of households were found with husband having graduate and above. Thus, educational levels of male couples were found low in this district, despite literacy level were very high (85.2%). As implied by illiterate row of Table–2.10, among the sub-divisions, Chandel sub-division had highest literacy rate of husband (94.6%) followed by Tengnoupal (87.1%), Machi (83.9%) and Chakpikarong (78.8%) respectively. It is also interesting to note that Chakpikarong male couple (13.6) had the highest educational level while lowest percentage (8.1) of male couple in Chandel possessed the highest level of education. In the district, the percentage of households with the female couple having literate but under matriculate were as high as 46.4. Like male couple, percentage of households with literate was high 79.2 but only 4.7% of households with female couple had educational level of graduate and above.

While discussing educational level of female couple by sub-division it was found that the female couple with illiterates was found highest in Chakpikarong (25.5) and lowest in Machi (16.7). But interestingly, it was also found that the percentage of households with female couple who attained the highest educational level (graduate and above) was found in Machi (5.6) and the lowest was found in Tengnoupal (3.6).

Table–3.10
Sub-Division wise distribution of educational level of couple

Factor	Category	Sub-Division				Total
		Tengn-oupal	Machi	Chandel	Chakpi-karong	
Educa-tional level of husband	Illiterate	36 (12.9) 36	27 (16.1)	13 (5.4)	83 (21.2)	159 (14.8)

	Literate but under matriculate	154 (54.5)	77 (47.1)	119 (51.4)	179 (45.5)	533 (49.8)
	Matriculate but below 10+2	39 (13.9)	34 (20.7)	69 (29.7)	54 (13.6)	192 (17.9)
	10+2 but under graduate	17 (5.9)	9 (5.7)	12 (5.4)	24 (6.1)	62 (5.8)
	Graduate and above	36 (12.9)	17 (10.3)	19 (8.1)	53 (13.6)	125 (11.7)
	Total	282 (100)	164 (100)	232 (100)	393 (100)	1071 (100)
Educational level of wife	Illiterate	60 (21.4)	27 (16.7)	42 (18.5)	100 (25.5)	223 (20.8)
	Literate but under matriculate	176 (62.5)	73 (44.4)	69 (29.6)	157 (40.0)	497 (46.4)
	Matriculate but below 10+2	30 (10.7)	37 (22.2)	94 (40.7)	64 (16.4)	212 (19.8)
	10+2 but under graduate	5 (1.8)	18 (11.1)	17 (7.4)	50 (12.7)	89 (8.3)
	Graduate and above	10 (3.6)	9 (5.6)	9 (3.7)	22 (5.5)	50 (4.7)
	Total	282 (100)	164 (100)	232 (100)	393 (100)	1071 (100)

3.10e Distribution of Students by Educational Parameters

In Table–3.11, the population under study was distributed according to some intended parameters of education – type of educational institution, means of travelling to school, and number of dropout children. It was interestingly observed that 66.8 of students studied in private schools and colleges and the rest 33.2% in government. The similar pattern was also seen in all four sub-divisions. The highest percentage of the students who went to private institution was found in Machi (68.9) which was followed by Chandel (67.7). It was shown that 61.6 of students went to school on foot in the district. The rest 38.4% of them were travelling by other means – Van, Bus, Auto-rickshaw etc. Travelling on foot was highest in Chakpikarong (81.5) and followed by Machi (58.5). The same table also reveals percentage of students drop out by number of child. The table clearly shows that nearly 52.1% of households had no any drop out (nearly 48% of students had drop out). While 18.7% households had one drop out children and 20.9%, two drop out children, 8.3% had at least three drop out children in the surveyed population. An approximately similar pattern of the variation of drop-out children was noted in all four sub-divisions and also in both boys and girls. However, the highest proportion (12.7%) of households with more than three drop-out children was found in Machi sub-division and that of the lowest figure 6.6% was found in Chakpikarong sub-division. To see the socio-economic development of a district/region, health care factors are also investigated. Only three interested factors were considered in the study. They are source of drinking water, type of toilet/latrine used and major means of cooking.

Table–3.11
Sub-division wise distribution of students by educational parameters

Factor	Category	Sub-Division				Total
		Tengn-oupal	Machi	Chandel	Chakpi-karong	
Types of institution	Govt.	97 (34.4)	51 (31.1)	75 (32.3)	133 (33.8)	356 (33.2)
	Private	185 (65.6)	113 (68.9)	157 (67.7)	260 (66.2)	715 (66.8)
	Total	282 (100)	164 (100)	232 (100)	393 (100)	1071 (100)
Means of travelling to school	On foot	159 (56.5)	96 (58.5)	121 (52.2)	320 (81.5)	660 (61.6)
	Others	123 (43.5)	68 (41.5)	111 (47.8)	73 (18.5)	411 (38.4)
	Total	282 (100)	164 (100)	232 (100)	393 (100)	1071 (100)

No. of drop out children	Nil	138 (49.1)	83 (50.8)	112 (48.3)	224 (57.0)	558 (52.1)
	1	58 (20.4)	31 (19.0)	39 (16.9)	73 (18.5)	200 (18.7)
	2	63 (22.2)	29 (17.5)	63 (27.0)	70 (17.9)	224 (20.9)
	3+	23 (8.3)	21 (12.7)	18 (7.9)	26 (6.6)	89 (8.3)
	Total	282 (100)	164 (100)	232 (100)	393 (100)	1071 (100)

In this district only 22.4% of households had the facility of drinking water from pipe (Table–3.12). Other remaining 77.6% of household had their drinking water from underground (13.9), well (18.5), pond (14.6) and rivers and others (30.7). Thus, the people of Chandel District mainly depend on non-hygienic source of drinking water particularly river and others.

Table–3.12

Sub-division wise distribution of health related factors

Factor	Category	Sub-Division				Total
		Tengnoupal	Machi	Chandel	Chakpikarong	
Source of drinking water	Pipe	39 (13.8)	62 (38.0)	46 (20.0)	44 (11.1)	240 (22.4)
	Underground	47 (16.7)	21 (12.7)	23 (10.0)	53 (13.6)	149 (13.9)
	Well	86 (30.4)	27 (16.2)	23 (10.0)	29 (7.4)	198 (18.5)
	Pond	26 (9.4)	15 (9.2)	33 (14.0)	131 (33.3)	156 (14.6)
	River and others	84 (29.7)	39 (23.9)	107 (46.0)	136 (34.6)	329 (30.7)
	Total	282 (100)	164 (100)	232 (100)	393 (100)	1071 (100)
Type of toilet/ latrine used	Pucca/ Sanitary	43 (15.2)	31 (18.9)	41 (17.7)	65 (16.5)	180 (7.8)
	Local/ Own made	196 (69.6)	125 (76.2)	177 (76.3)	319 (81.2)	817 (84.2)

	Open/ Jungle & others	43 (15.2)	8 (4.9)	14 (6.0)	9 (2.3)	74 (8.0)
	Total	282 (100)	164 (100)	232 (100)	393 (100)	1071 (100)
Major means of cooking	Petroleum gas	80 (28.3)	23 (14.1)	42 (18.0)	44 (11.1)	200 (18.7)
	Others	202 (71.7)	141 (85.9)	190 (82.0)	349 (88.9)	871 (81.3)
	Total	282 (100)	164 (100)	232 (100)	393 (100)	1071 (100)

Drinking water facility from pipe was found highest in Machi sub-division (38.0) and lowest in Chakpikarong sub-division (11.1). The percentage of households which owned pucca toilet was only 7.8%, remaining 84.2% of households depended on local or own made toilet and another remaining 8% had open/single toilet. The percentage of households having pucca toilet was highest in Machi sub-division (18.9) and lowest in Tengnoupal (15.2) which was next to Chakpikarong (16.5). The same table also shows that the percentage of households having cooking gas facility was only 18.7 in the district. Such facility was highest in Tengnoupal (28.3) and lowest in Chakpikarong (11.1).

Table–3.13 shows the level of some intended demographic characters viz., women's age at marriage, women's age at first delivery, number of live birth ever born to a couple and number of children born alive but now deceased. In this district 15.3% of women were married before reaching the legal age of marriage (18 years) and only 9.5% of them had late marriage that is after 30 year of their age. The highest proportion of 33.3% of women married during their early age 18-20 years. The similar pattern of variation was noted in all sub-divisions under investigation. Early child marriage was highest in Machi followed by that in Tengnoupal.

Table–3.13
Sub-Division wise distribution of important demographic factors

Factor	Category	Sub-Division				Total
		Tengnoupal	Machi	Chandel	Chakpikarong	
Women' age (in yr) at marriage	<18	45 (15.9)	32 (19.7)	33 (14.0)	29 (7.4)	161 (15.3)
	18-20	92 (32.6)	46 (28.2)	74 (32.0)	175 (44.4)	357 (33.3)
	21-23	63 (22.5)	30 (18.3)	23 (10.0)	102 (25.9)	216 (20.2)
	24-26	41 (14.5)	31 (19.0)	46 (20.0)	34 (8.6)	167 (15.6)
	27-29	14 (5.1)	12 (7.0)	19 (8.0)	19 (4.9)	65 (6.1)
	30+	27 (9.5)	13 (7.7)	37 (16.0)	34 (8.6)	102 (9.5)
Women's age (in yr) at first delivery	<18	43 (15.2)	30 (18.3)	37 (16.0)	19 (4.9)	154 (14.4)
	18-20	20 (7.2)	19 (11.3)	32 (14.0)	121 (30.9)	151 (14.1)
	21-23	141 (50.0)	65 (39.4)	74 (32.0)	155 (39.5)	450 (42.1)
	24-26	45 (15.9)	29 (17.6)	37 (16.0)	44 (11.1)	167 (15.6)
	27-29	10 (3.6)	13 (7.7)	14 (6.0)	20 (4.9)	60 (5.6)
	30+	23 (8.0)	9 (5.6)	38 (16.0)	34 (8.6)	89 (8.3)
No. of live birth ever born to a couple	At most 2	117 (41.5)	65 (39.4)	77 (33.3)	99 (25.3)	392 (36.6)
	3-4	84 (29.6)	66 (40.1)	92 (39.6)	159 (40.5)	392 (36.6)
	5-6	63 (22.2)	25 (15.3)	58 (25.0)	90 (22.8)	217 (20.3)
	7+	19 (6.7)	8 (5.1)	5 (2.1)	45 (11.4)	70 (6.5)

No. of children born alive but now deceased	Nil	256 (90.6)	149 (90.8)	213 (92.0)	345 (87.7)	967 (90.3)
	One	16 (5.8)	13 (7.7)	9 (4.0)	29 (7.4)	71 (6.6)
	At least two	10 (3.6)	2 (1.4)	10 (4.0)	19 (4.9)	34 (3.2)
	Total	282 (100)	164 (100)	232 (100)	393 (100)	1071 (100)

As per pattern of the variation in age at marriage, the women's age at first delivery is concentrated in the age group of 21-23 years in the sense that most of women in the population (42.1%) delivered their first birth in the age range of 21-23 year. From this nature of variation in age at marriage and age at first delivery, it may be concluded that most of the women's first birth interval (time interval between marriage and first birth) is approaching to one year. Taking the current birth performance or so called current fertility, only 36.6% of the couples in surveyed population had at most two live birth and another 36.6% had 2-3 live birth. Out of remaining, 20.3% had 5-6 live births and 6.5% had at least 7 live births. Among the four sub-divisions the highest percentage of couples was found to have more seven live births in Chakpikarong which was followed by that of Tengnoupal. The present findings highlighted that the national target of replacement fertility of 2.1 children may not be achieved in the district. In case of child mortality, about 10% of the surveyed households had experience of no child mortality. It also indicates that national target or child mortality control cannot be achieved in Chandel district.

To sum up, the topographic features, demographic characteristics, distribution of main workers, agricultural parameters, literate family members, educational level of couple, students by educational parameters, etc. clearly show that the development of Chandel district might be influenced by the socio-economic conditions of the district.

4

Chapter

Socio-Economic Determinants of Family Income

4.1 Introduction

The future social development is usually influenced by the present income. The size of present income is one of the major factors in determining the level of saving and capital formation which was considered as an engine of economic growth in various economic growth models such as in Balance Growth Theory of Rosenstein-Rodan and Ranger Nurkse, and Neo-classical growth theory of Harrod-Domar. At micro economic level, higher family income is very much essential not only for saving and investment for physical capital but also for human capital which are crucial for attainment of future economic growth of a family as well as an economy. In this context, an investigation into the variation in the family income level with respect to some interested socio-economic and demographic characters may be fascinating to a considerable extent. Here, the considered factors are place of residence, type of family, size of family, number of family members engaged in agricultural and allied activities, educational level, employment status, standard of living, age at marriage, age at delivery, number of deceased children etc.

4.1.1 Test Statistics

When testing whether the average family income, measured in terms of arithmetic mean of selected two samples drawn from the study population is significantly different or not, it assumes: (a) a normal (Gaussian) distribution for the populations of the random errors, and (b) there is no significant difference between the standard deviations of both population samples. The two means and the corresponding standard deviations are computed by using the following equations. Here, n_A and n_B are the number of eligible couples in data set A and data set B respectively.

$$\overline{X}_A = \frac{\sum_{i=1}^{n_A} X_i}{n_A}, \qquad \overline{X}_B = \frac{\sum_{i=1}^{n_B} X_i}{n_B}$$

$$S_A = \sqrt{\frac{\sum_{i=1}^{n_A}\left(X_i - \overline{X}_A\right)^2}{n_A - 1}}, \qquad S_B = \sqrt{\frac{\sum_{i=1}^{n_B}\left(X_i - \overline{X}_B\right)^2}{n_B - 1}}$$

Then, the pooled estimate of standard deviation S_{AB} is computed as

$$S_{AB} = \sqrt{\frac{(n_A - 1)S_A{}^2 + (n_B - 1)S_B{}^2}{n_A - n_B - 2}}$$

Finally, the statistic t_{exp} read asexperimental t value is defined by

$$t_{exp} = \frac{\left|\overline{X}_A - \overline{X}_B\right|}{S_{AB}\sqrt{\frac{1}{n_A} + \frac{1}{n_B}}}$$

"texp" value is compared with the critical (theoretical) t_{th} value corresponding to the given degree of freedom N ($N = n_A + n_B - 2$) at 95% confidence level (CI). If $t_{exp} > t_{th}$ then H_0 is rejected else H_0 is retained. Instead of test value, it is advocated by P-values. When comparing the average family income of more than two samples, F-test may be applied. In this context, samples are defined by different categories or classes of an independent variable or factor say for instance, name of tribes in the study population are Kuki, Chothe, Maring, Lamkang, Tarao, Moyon, Monsang, Anal etc. These tribes may be treated as different samples in the present analysis. The 'F'–test statistics is given by

$$F = \frac{S_B/(k-1)}{S_W/(n-k)}$$

Follows F-distribution with (k-1, n-k) d.f

where, $S_B/(k-1)$ is called Between Samples Mean Sum of Square while,
$S_W/(n-k)$ is called Error Mean Sum of Square.

4.1.2 Significance Level

The rejection or acceptance of the null hypotheses is checked by P-values and possible range of the estimated statistics of average family income in the present investigation is explored in terms of 95% confidence interval (CI). The analysis is based on observed field data of 1071 surveyed family in the population under study.

4.1.3 P-Value

While investigating the variations in the average family income a disadvantage of choosing in advance, a level of significance of say, 5% of 't' and 'F' may close or far from the cutoff, and the degree of closeness is not indicated. An alternative is to present the P-value (also known as the probability value of observed level of significance) or exact level of significance or exact probability of committing type I error. The P-value is the test level that would just hereby allow rejection of null hypothesis, H_0 given the test-value is calculated from the sample. In other words, P value may be defined as the lowest significance level at which a null hypothesis can be rejected. It is the probability of observing a test-value at least as extreme as the test-value calculated from the sample, under the assumption that H_0 is true. Since P-values are probability, they range between 0 and 1. A low P-value is a number near 0, and a high P-value is a number near 1. A low P-value indicates a high observed level of statistical significance, and a high P-value indicates a low observed level of statistical significance. However, 0.05 is taken as cutoff statistical significance level and 0.01 is that high significance level in the present analysis.

4.1.4 Confidence Intervals (CI)

The estimated parameter from a sample gives a single (point) estimate of the un-known population. Because of sampling fluctuations, single estimate is likely to vary from that of population value, though mean of repeated sampling is expected to be equal to true value. As a result of this an interval around point estimator is reasonable.

Using the definition of t distribution, we know that

$$\Pr(-t_{0.25} < t < t_{0.25}) = 0.95 \qquad \text{(i)}$$

where 'Pr' denotes probability. Allowing that β may be non zero, and substituting $(b-\beta)/s_b$ for t, we can rewrite (i) as

$$P_r\left(-t_{0.25} < \frac{b-\beta}{S_b} < t_{0.25}\right) = 0.95 \qquad \text{(ii)}$$

If we multiply the string of inequalities within parentheses by S_b, subtract b, multiply by -1 (thereby reversing the direction of the inequalities), and then flip the string of inequalities around, (ii) becomes

$$\Pr(b - t_{0.25}S_b < \beta < b + t_{0.25}S_b) = 0.95 \qquad \text{(iii)}$$

Equivalently,The 95%CI for β is $b \pm t_{0.25}S_b$ (iv)

where b is the estimate of derived from our particular sample. Equation (iii) and statement (iv) say that there is a 95% probability (we are 95% confident) that the interval includes β. Again, $t_{0.25}$ is not computed from the data but is looked up in the prescribed table (Standard Normal Cumulative Probability) with d.f = n-2. The 95% confidence interval may be viewed as an interval estimate of β. The size of the interval is a measure of the precision of the estimate. The wide of the confidence interval is proportional to the standard error of the estimator. To be specific, the larger is standard error, the larger is the width of the interval. In other words, this larger value of the estimator implies the higher level of uncertainty of estimating the true value of unknown parameter.

4.2 Family Income according to Place of Residence and Sub-Division

Differential in socio-economic development is associated with rural-urban classes in India. In one sense, urbanization stands for growth of non-agricultural activities. It is associated with growth of industrialization, trade and commerce. Out of total population 29.21 percent was found in the urban area constituting 51 towns (28 statutory and 23 census towns) in Manipur according to 2011 census. It witnesses that the process of urbanization has been very slow in the state which perhaps indicates a slower occupational shift. Place of residence is one of the socio-economic factors affecting level of reproductive performance which determines people's life styles, their perceptions of the global context, economic, social, cultural and political activities. In this country, urban-rural difference transcends in importance many other social and economic characteristics. The concept of urban residence as understood in the West is different from the context of Manipur society. Even if the couples have urban residence, they often continue to have link with rural areas by way of economic interest, social and cultural ties there. However, the differential in the family income has been analysed with respect to place of residence in the present section.

Table–4.1
Differential monthly income (in Rs.) according to place of residence

Place of residence	No. of house-holds (%)	Mean ± S.D	95%CI for mean	Test values
Rural	941 (87.9)	12696 ± 15448	11090-14301	t=1.67,
Urban	130 (12.1)	8944 ± 8523	6496-11392	P>0.05
Total	**1071 (100)**	**12244 ± 14830**	**10799–13689**	

In this analysis, the urban-rural differential is defined according to Population of Manipur, 2006 (Directorate of Economics and Statistic, Govt. of Manipur, 2008). It may be observed from Table–4.1 that the proportion of surveyed families in urban and rural areas were 12% and 88%

respectively. Irrespective of the effects of other factors, the average family income in urban area was observed to be Rs. 8944 ± 8523 with 95% CI: 6496-11392 and that of rural area, Rs. 12696 ± 15448 with 95% CI of 11090-14301 while the overall average income of the study population, Rs. 12244±14830 (95% CI: 10799-13689). Though there is visible difference, it was found statistically insignificant variation in the family income according to place of residence. It was witnessed by t-value (1.67, P>0.05) in the population. This insignificance is due to lack of urban characteristics in urban areas of Chandel district. Urban-rural distinction is not very clear here, unlike other advanced states as mentioned above. The variation in the income level is also investigated according to different sub-divisions in the population in this section.

Table–4.2
Differential monthly income (in Rs.) according to Sub-Division

Sub-Division	No. of house-holds (%)	Mean ± S.D	95%CI for mean	Test values
Tengnoupal	360 (33.6)	15384 ± 16027	12646-18123	F=3.09,
Machi	369 (34.5)	10905 ± 13519	8662-13148	P<0.05
Chandel	131 (12.2)	9937 ± 12148	6484-13389	
Chakpikarong	211 (19.7)	10820 ± 15860	7313-14327	
Total	**1071 (100)**	**12244 ± 14830**	**10799-13689**	

Chandel as stated above has four sub-divisions namely Tengnoupal (33.6%), Machi (34.5%), Chandel (12.2%) and Chakpikarong (19.7%) manifested in Table–4.2. The highest family income of Rs. 15384 ± 16027 with 95% CI: 12646-18123 was observed in Tengnoupal and the lowest level of Rs. 9937 ± 12148 (95% CI: 6484-13389) was found in Chandel while the overall average income was Rs. 12244 ± 14830 with 95% CI: 10799-13689. This distribution of the average income was statistically significant with four categories of sub-divisions without considering the effects of other factors under investigation, as advocated by F-statistics (3.09, P<0.05). The reason for high income in the Tengnoupal might perhaps be due to the fact that the people of the sub-division are having business attitude. Some of them have engaged in various business activities in the International Border Town at Moreh. In the case of Chandel the main activities of the people are agriculture and hence, it has low income.

4.3 Family Income according to Type of Family

In the family system in India, the institution of joint family or so called extended family and nuclear family are considered to be one of the important factors influencing on income of the family. But in the context of Manipur, particularly Chandel district it might not be true because the family set-up in the district is different from that of western society. A considerable proportion of nuclear family's households has spent substantial period of time in joint families before formation of nuclear families of their own in Manipur. The nuclear families in Western sense or proper sense are supposed to be quite negligible in Indian Societies, particularly in Manipur societies. In the present investigation, the nuclear family refers to residentially nuclear families and it may be treated as the family consisting of husband, wife and their own children only. All types of family other than nuclear family may be considered as joint family.

Table–4.3
Differential monthly income (in Rs.) according to type of family

Type of Family	No. of house-holds (%)	Mean ± S.D	95%CI for mean	Test values
Nuclear	1037 (96.8)	12007 ± 14719	10549-13464	t=1.78,
Joint	34 (3.2)	19438 ± 16978	9178-29697	P>0.05
Total	**1071 (100)**	**12244 ± 14830**	**10799-13689**	

The 97% of the total family belongs to nuclear family and the rest, only 3% to joint family (Table–4.3) in the population. The average income level of joint family was found to be Rs. 19438 ± 16978 with 95% CI: 9178-29697 which was higher than that of nuclear family, Rs. 12007 ± 14719 with 95% CI: 10549-13464. The variation in the mean monthly family income according to type of family was statistically insignificant (t=1.78, P>0.05). It may be concluded that there is no significant difference in the family income between joint family and nuclear ones in the population irrespective of the effects of other factors under investigation. The insignificant difference may be caused by the family set ups of Manipur, particularly the present hill areas. As stated above, the couples have adopted nuclear family after spending a considerable duration of time with their parents as joint family.

4.4 Family Income according to Community

The religious or community diversity has caused to lack of sustainable development in India. It has contributed to heterogeneous socio-demographic indices which are again linked with economic development of a state too. Social stratification by caste system practiced in the state is not strict as done in many parts of the country. The Meities – original inhabitants of Manipur, the Brahmins, the scheduled caste, and scheduled tribe have adopted to live together in various parts of the State. Moreover, in contrast to the caste prejudices in some other parts of India the schedule caste and schedule tribe are not untouchable sections of the population in the community. In other words, there is no practically untouchable community in the state of Manipur and there is no caste distinction in the state as found in other parts of India.

In this small section, the variation in the average family income level has been investigated according to different tribes/communities residing in the district under study. For analysis purpose, nine different communities are included. They are Kuki, Chothe, Maring, Lamkang, Tarao, Moyon, Monsang, Anal, and Non-Local/Tribal.

Table–4.4
Differential monthly income (in Rs.) according to name of tribes/community

Name of tribes/ Community	No. of house-holds (%)	Mean ± S.D	95%CI for mean	Test values
Kuki	305 (28.5)	11059 ± 13946	8460-13658	F=1.49,

Chothe	127 (11.9)	11619 ± 16402	2879-20359	P>0.05
Maring	169 (15.8)	12913 ± 14529	10751-15074	
Lamkang	76 (7.1)	14059 ± 18002	4803-23314	
Tarao	52 (4.9)	4939 ± 5535	2422-8456	
Moyon	56 (5.2)	6211 ± 6252	2433-9989	
Monsang	71 (6.6)	16280 ± 13289	8921-23640	
Anal	130 (12.1)	17452 ± 22772	8790-26114	
Non-Local/ Tribal	85 (7.9)	9112 ± 7954	4874-13350	
Total	**1071 (100)**	**12244 ± 14830**	**10799-13689**	

From the empirical findings, it was observed that the family income level of Anal tribe was highest say Rs. 17452 ± 22772 with 95% CI of Rs. 8790-26114 which was followed by Monsang with Rs. 16280 ± 13289 (95% CI: 8921-23640) and the lowest level of Rs. 4939 ± 5535 with 95% CI: 2422-8456 was observed in Tarao tribe (Table–4.4). One of the important findings was that the non-locals or so called non-tribes had lower income level (Rs. 9112 ± 7954 with 95% CI: 4874-13350) in the population. It might be due to the fact that most of the non-tribal people are residing in the district purposively for small business. Without considering the effects of other factors under investigation, the variation in the average family income levels was found to be statistically insignificant according to nine tribes or communities (F=1.49, P>0.05).

Table–4.5
Differential monthly income (in Rs.) according to religion

Religion	No. of house-holds (%)	Mean ± S.D	95%CI for mean	Test values
Christian	1035 (96.6)	12402 ± 14989	10915-13888	t=1.14,
Non-Christian	36 (3.4)	7809 ± 8502	2900-12717	P>0.05
Total	**1071 (100)**	**12244 ± 14830**	**10799-13689**	

The insignificance income differentiation of these tribes is clearly explained by the fact that the earnings of these tribes are mainly influenced by topographic features of the district. Since they are living in the same topographical features their income would not be much different. Moreover, their work attitudes are also almost the same. Apart from the statistical significance, the income level of Anal community was comparatively high. One of the most possible causes of it may be the community has a good number of government employees. It may again be influenced by political advantages. In contrast with it, the reason for low income of the Tarao community may be due to the fact that they have less government employees and most of their livelihood has depended on the traditional agriculture say, shifting cultivation and handicraft which have low income generation.

Differentiating the families under investigation by their religion category, the income level of Rs. 7809 ± 8502 with 95% CI of Rs. 2900-12717 for non-Christian families was visibly lower than that of Christian families, Rs. 12402 ± 14989 with 95% CI of Rs. 10915-13888 (Table–4.5). The variation is statistically insignificant, as advocated by its test (t) value, 1.14 at 5% probability level of significance. Majority of Chandel population embrace the Christian faith. Non-Christians were in minority. Christian missionaries brought not only Christianity but also development in education. Many educational institutions were established in every sub-division. Most of the students studied in these institutions. It may also be mentioned that in recent years many other private institutions were also established. Naturally, Christian children were more educated than non-Christian. Hence, most of the job opportunities either in government departments or private institutions goes to Christianity group. As such, the income level of Christian was higher than non-Christian, despite the difference was insignificant. The reason for insignificance is the same as explained in section 4.4.

4.5 Family Income according to Size of Family

In many countries, family size plays a role on the household income levels due to many reasons. Two-person families have lower incomes; that owes to the fact that many of these families are young couples starting out in life or single parents drawing only one pay check. The same logic follows for three-person families. Past findings have shown that families are not able to maintain per capita income, per capita expenditures and per capita savings as family size increase. The families are also not able to maintain per capita expenditure on human capital as family size increases. It has also shown that there is a strong and enduring link between poverty incidence and vulnerability to poverty and family size in the sense that larger family size is associated with higher poverty incidence, gap and severity.

In the present small section, the family income levels have been analysed with respect to the size of family which is defined by the number of persons or so called family members in the surveyed households. The differential in family income was observed to be statistically insignificant according to the size of family, as $F=1.52, P>0.05$. A similar pattern of variation was also found in the case of the size of male family member in the population (Table–4.7). However, the family income varies significantly with the number of female family member as evidenced by $F = 4.02, P<0.05$ irrespective of the effects of other factors under consideration. The inverse correlation between family income and number of female family member beyond the one female family member was observed in Table–4.8. In the population, the income levels visibly varies in non-linear pattern according to number of family member, number of male family member and also number of female family member.

Table–4.6
Differential monthly income (in Rs.) according to size of family

Size of Family	No. of house-holds (%)	Mean ± S.D	95%CI for mean	Test values
<3	47 (4.4)	6771 ± 13904	1436-13685	F=1.52,
3-5	508 (47.4)	13517 ± 16872	11122-15912	P>0.05
6-8	433 (40.4)	11314 ± 12212	9437-13191	

>8	83 (7.8)	12445 ± 14023	7301-17588
Total	**1071 (100)**	**12244 ± 14830**	**10799-13689**

Table–4.7
Differential monthly income (in Rs.) according to size of male family member

Size of Male Member	No. of households (%)	Mean ± S.D	95%CI for mean	Test values
At most 1	155 (14.5)	9240 ± 13324	5737-12743	F=0.79,
2	370 (34.5)	13257 ± 15112	10741-15773	P>0.05
3	273 (25.5)	12719 ± 16368	9551-15886	
4	174 (16.3)	12148 ± 13238	8894-15402	
At least 5	99 (9.2)	11915 ± 14195	7182-16648	
Total	**1071 (100)**	**12244 ± 14830**	**10799-13689**	

While differentiated the income with number of family member, the highest income (Rs. 13517 ± 16872 with 95% CI: 11122-15912) was observed in the family of size 3-5 members (47.4%) which was followed by Rs. 12445 ± 14023 in the family of size eight and above members (7.8%) and the lowest level (Rs. 6771 ± 13904 with 95% CI: 1436-13685) was noted in the family of size below 3 members (4.4%) shown in Table–4.6. In the case of differentiated the family income with the number of male family member, the highest income, say Rs. 13257 ± 15112 (95% CI: 10741-15773) was found in the family having two male members (34.5%) followed by Rs. 12719 ± 16368 with 95% CI: 9551-15886 in the family with three male family members (25.5%) noted in Table–4.7. The lowest income of Rs. 9240 ± 13324 was noted in the family with at most one male member (14.5%) while overall average of the family income was Rs. 12244 ± 14830 with its 95% CI: 10799-13689 in the population under investigation. The highest income level of Rs. 15735 ± 18951 (95% CI: 12521-18949) was also observed in the family having only two female members and the lowest level of Rs. 7456 ± 9123 (95% CI: 5079-9834) was noted in the family with at most one female member (Table–4.8). Here also, the pattern of variation in the family income has non linear trend according to the size of female family members in the study population.

Table–4.8
Differential monthly income (in Rs.) according to size of female family member

Size of Female Member	No. of house-holds (%)	Mean ± S.D	95%CI for mean	Test values
At most 1	154 (14.4)	7456 ± 9123	5079-9834	F=4.02,
2	357 (33.3)	15735 ± 18951	12521-18949	P<0.05
3	264 (24.6)	11199 ± 12365	8720-13678	
4	169 (15.8)	10178 ± 10374	7608-12749	
At least 5	127 (11.9)	13150 ± 15022	8835-17465	
Total	**1071 (100)**	**12244 ± 14830**	**10799-13689**	

4.6 Family Income according to Education

To investigate the relationship between education and family income, the present section has been introduced. In the present study educational level is measured in terms of number of literate persons, number of male literate family members, number of female literate family members and educational level of couple. In the empirical data, it was observed that there was positive associations between educational level of the family and the income level (Table–4.9 to Table–4.13). In this analysis, the number of literate person in the family is grouped in the four categories – below 2, 2-3, 4-5 and 6 and above. The highest family income of Rs. 15050 ± 15908 with 95 %CI: 11532-18568 was found in the category of 6 literates and above followed by that of 4-5 literate persons category (Rs. 14565 ± 15703 with 95% CI: 12056-17073) and the lowest income, Rs. 6896 ± 11070 with 95% CI: 3150-10641 in below 2 literate persons in the family while overall average of the family income of the population was Rs. 12244 ± 14830 with its 95% CI: 10799-13689 (Table–4.9). This variation in the income level according to the number of literate persons in the family was observed to be highly significant as witnessed by the value of F-statistics, 5.71

($P<0.01$) irrespective of the effects of other factors under consideration.

Table–4.9
Differential monthly income (in Rs.) according to literate persons in the family

No. of person	No. of house-holds (%)	Mean ± S.D	95%CI for mean	Test values
<2	94 (8.8)	6896 ± 11070	3150-10641	F=5.71,
2-3	357 (33.3)	9305 ± 13269	7047-11564	P<0.01
4-5	406 (37.9)	14565 ± 15703	12056-17073	
6+	214 (20.0)	15050 ± 15908	11532-18568	
Total	**1071 (100)**	**12244 ± 14830**	**10799-13689**	

Table–4.10
Differential monthly income (in Rs.) according to male literate family member

No. of Male Member	No. of house-holds (%)	Mean ± S.D	95%CI for mean	Test values
At most 1	341 (31.8)	8544 ± 10599	6704-10383	r=0.15,
2	367 (34.3)	14551 ± 17639	11603-17498	P<0.01
3	232 (21.7)	11924 ± 13581	9046-14801	F=4.01,
4	89 (8.3)	14757 ± 15526	9340-20175	P<0.01
At least 5	42 (3.9)	18967 ± 17160	9464-28470	
Total	**1071 (100)**	**12244 ± 14830**	**10799-13689**	

Though having a visibly non-linear relations between family income and the number of male literate family member, a positive relationship between the two variables was observed as evidenced by the value of correlation coefficient say $r=0.15$ ($P<0.01$) without considering the effects of other variables under investigation (Table–4.10). The variation in the income levels was also found to be significant with different categories of the number of male literates in the family ($F=4.01$, $P<0.01$). However, the variation in the family income was insignificantly different with respect to the number of female literates ($P>0.05$)

highlighted in Table–4.11. The positive and significant relation between income and male literate family member reveal the male dominance in the tribal society of Chandel.

Table–4.11
Differential monthly income (in Rs.) according to female literate family member

No. of Female Member	No. of house-holds (%)	Mean ± S.D	95%CI for mean	Test values
At most 1	467 (43.6)	10167 ± 14046	8089-12245	r=0.09,
2	320 (29.9)	15112 ± 16638	12117-18107	P>0.05
3	172 (16.1)	12633 ± 14151	9126-16139	F=2.21,
4	86 (7.8)	11082 ± 9207	7763-14402	P>0.05
At least 5	29 (2.7)	15385 ± 19457	2314-28456	
Total	**1071 (100)**	**12244 ± 14830**	**10799-13689**	

In this section, it is also checked the variation in the income level according to educational levels of both spouses. Here, the educational achievement of spouses is categorized into five levels – illiterate, under matriculate, matriculate, 10+2 standard, and graduate and above. In the distribution of the family income with respect to educational level of male spouse, it was noted that the highest mean family income of Rs. 22852 ± 18396 with 95% CI: 13394-32310 was found in the graduate and above category followed by Rs. 22652 ± 21183 with 95% CI: 15261-30044 in the 10+2 standard category and the lowest income of Rs. 9966 ± 12317 with 95% CI: 7945-11988 was found in literate but below matriculate category. The variation in the average family income was significant with education of male spouses, as evidenced by F-statistics (7.48) at 1% level of significance (P<0.01) shown in Table - 4.12. This confirms the general finding that there is higher earning capacity of persons with higher level of education. From this analysis, it may be highlighted that family income is directly associated with educational achievement of male spouses in the district. In the visible count, the family income was also improved with upward changing in educational level of female spouses. However, the variation in the average family income was found to be statistically insignificant ($F=1.88, P>0.05$) with respect to the educational achievement of female spouse in the population under consideration (Table–4.13).

Table–4.12
Differential monthly income (in Rs.) according to educational level of male spouse

Educational level	No. of households (%)	Mean ± S.D	95%CI for mean	Test values
Illiterate	159 (14.8)	10886 ± 12544	6977-14795	F=7.48, P<0.01
Literate but under matriculate	533 (49.8)	9966 ± 12317	7945-11988	
Matriculate but below 10+2	192 (17.9)	15330 ± 16774	10612-20048	
10+2 but under graduate	62 (5.8)	22652 ± 21183	15261-30044	
Graduate and above	125 (11.7)	22852 ± 18396	13394-32310	
Total	**1071 (100)**	**12244 ± 14830**	**10799-13689**	

Comparing the patterns of variations in the mean family income according to couple's educational level, it is further be observed that the education of male spouse played a more significant role than that of the female spouse in improving the family income level. It may perhaps be due to the fact that most of the female spouses may engage in household work rather than government job having good salary income. Moreover, since male dominates female in this tribal district male education has more important role for creating higher income of couple in the family. This inference is, however, drawn without considering the joint effects of other factors under investigation.

Table–4.13
Differential monthly income (in Rs.) according to educational level of female spouse

Educational Level	No. of households (%)	Mean ± S.D	95%CI for mean	Test values
Illiterate	223 (20.8)	8366 ± 9108	5453-11279	F=1.88,
Literate but under matriculate	497 (46.4)	13679 ± 18820	9692-17667	P>0.05
Matriculate but below 10+2	212 (19.8)	11162 ± 9336	8093-14231	
10+2 but under graduate	89 (8.3)	12357 ± 13330	5255-19460	
Graduate and above	50 (4.7)	22010 ± 14695	10715-33305	
Total	**1071 (100)**	**12244 ± 14830**	**10799-13689**	

4.7 Family Income according to Agriculture and Allied Activities

The people of Manipur primarily depend on agriculture and allied activities. Traditionally, people in the hill areas cultivate on high slopes and abandon the plots after a few years in the practice of jhuming or shifting cultivation. Arable land for terrace cultivation is marginal and hence agriculture has persistently been on subsistence level in Chandel district, Manipur. In Manipur, agriculture sector also contributes a major share to the total state domestic product and provided employment to about 57.04% of the total workers in 2013-14. The state domestic product has fluctuated depending on the performance of agriculture sector. Notwithstanding, the crucial importance of this primary sector in the hill economy too, the irregular and erratic behavior of monsoon accompanied by inadequate irrigation facilities have resulted in severe fluctuations in agricultural production. Thus, in this section, it aims to examine the variation in the family income levels according to the number of family members engaged in agriculture and allied activities.

Table–4.14
Differential monthly income (in Rs.) according to number of family members

No. of person engaged	No. of house-holds (%)	Mean ± S.D	95%CI for mean	Test values
<3	379 (35.4)	10155 ± 14107	7814-12495	F=3.07,
3-5	604 (6.4)	13279 ± 15263	11269-15289	P<0.05
6+	88 (8.2)	16231 ± 15329	10704-21757	
Total	**1071 (100)**	**12244 ± 14830**	**10799-13689**	

The surveyed families have been clubbed into three groups according to the number of family members engaged in agriculture and allied activities. They are below 3, 3-5, and 6 and above. The average family income is distributed according to these three classes (Table - 4.14). The highest family income, Rs. 16231 ± 15329 with 95% CI: 10704-21757 was observed among the families having at least six members engaged in agriculture and allied activities. It was followed by Rs. 13279 ± 15263 with 95% CI of Rs. 11269-15289 in the families with 3-5 members engaged in the agriculture. The lowest income of Rs. 10155 ± 14107 with 95% CI: 7814-12495 was observed in the families in which less than 3 members were engaged in the agriculture and allied activities while overall average of the family income of the population was Rs. 12244 ± 14830 with its 95% CI: 10799-13689. Without considering the effects of other variables, the variation in the income level was found to be statistically significant (P<0.05) with the number of family members engaged in the agriculture and allied activities in the population under study, as evidenced by the test value (F=3.07). In hilly areas cultivation of rice requires more labour for producing more production. As a result there is significant positive correlation between income and number of labour used.

4.8 Family Income according to Age at Marriage

It is also worth to note that consciousness of earning family income generally starts particularly from the time of their marriage. Therefore, the variation in the family income has been analysed with respect to female age at marriage in the population. For analysis purpose, the female spouses have been clubbed into six groups according to their completed ages at marriage. They are below 18 years, 18-20 years, 21-23 years, 24-26 years, 27-29 years and 30 years and above. The average family income is distributed according to age at marriage of female spouses in Table–4.15.

The highest family income, Rs. 17138 ± 24567 with 95% CI: 6997-27279 was observed among the family in which the women were married at the age of 27-29 years which constitutes only 6.1% of the surveyed population. It was followed by Rs. 14242 ± 16312 with 95% CI of Rs. 11476-17009 in those who married between 18-20 years of their completed age. While overall average of the family income of the population was Rs. 12244 ± 14830 with its 95% CI: 10799-13689,the very low income levels were observed in the family whose female spouses were married at the extreme class of below 18 years (Rs. 10356 ± 11723) and above 30 years (Rs. 8540 ± 12357). This variation in the income level was found to be statistically insignificant (P>0.05) with age at marriage of female spouse in the population, as evidenced by the test value (F=1.85). Though the relation is statistically insignificant, it is indicated that the younger age group (below 18 years of age) has little idea of earning while other age group (above 30 years of age) has no care of family life.

Table–4.15
Differential monthly income (in Rs.) according to female age at marriage

Age at marriage (in yr)	No. of house-holds (%)	Mean ± S.D	95%CI for mean	Test values
<18	164 (15.3)	10356 ± 11723	7379-13333	F=1.85,

18-20	357 (33.3)	14242 ± 16312	11476-17009	P>0.05
21-23	216 (20.2)	11281 ± 13678	8275-14286	
24-26	167 (5.6)	11348 ± 11048	8588-14108	
27-29	65 (6.1)	17138 ± 24567	6997-27279	
30+	102 (9.5)	8540 ± 12357	4478-12601	
Total	**1071 (100)**	**12244 ± 14830**	**10799-13689**	

4.9 Family Income according to Age at First Delivery

In India all births occur within the institution of marriage and proportion of illegitimate births is negligible. In fact, the raise in women age at marriage is a kind of birth control. It may be noted that by raising age at marriage of girls, natural reproductive span is cut down through higher age at delivery and therefore quantum of births could be reduced proportionately. Higher age at marriage and delivery would mean that they have more time to make career to earn more income. Women's age at first birth in developing countries has important consequences on the socio-demographic characters of population (Rajaretnam, 1990) as well as economic condition of them. A couple who intend to have one or two children may want to lengthen the spacing between marriage and first birth in order to establish their better life as a couple, and this would give more time for training and work experience before the first child arrives (Martin, 1995). Thus, the lengthening of the interval between marriage and first birth may be an important goal thereof, and it might also be in the interest of individual couples (Zheng, 2000). These various socio-economic repercussions of age of women at first delivery naturally would effect on the income of household in the district. On the basis of above discussion, it is justified to examine the relation between income and age of women at first delivery.

Table–4.16
Differential monthly income (in Rs.) according to age of women at first delivery

Age at delivery (in yr.)	No. of house-holds (%)	Mean ± S.D	95%CI for mean	Test values
<18	154 (14.4)	9702 ± 11365	6714-12691	F=1.53,
18-20	150 (14.0)	10826 ± 11623	7714-13939	P>0.05
21-23	451 (42.1)	14053 ± 16295	11600-16506	
24-26	167 (15.6)	10649 ± 10762	7961-13338	
27-29	60 (5.6)	15970 ± 25385	4992-26947	
30+	89 (8.3)	10244 ± 13434	5557-14932	
Total	**1071 (100)**	**12244 ± 14830**	**10799-13689**	

Though statistically insignificant difference (P>0.05) in the income levels of the surveyed population, some visible differences in the average income were observed according to the six categories of women's age at first delivery (Table–4.16). In this distribution, the highest average income of Rs. 15,970 ± 25385 with 95% CI: 4992-26947 and the lowest figure of Rs. 9702 ± 11365 with 95% CI: 6714-12691 were noted in the age group "27-29 year" and "below 18 year" respectively. In one sense, the age at delivery of mother may be considered a factor for determining family income. Because such delayed in child bearing has an implications in the earning capacity of the family.

4.10 Family Income and Number of Live Birth

It is well established fact in Manipur particularly hill areas that women participation in economic activities is one of the important socio-economic factors which influence on income. To check the effects of birth performance on the variation in family income level, the numbers of live birth ever born to a woman have been discussed. For analysis purpose, the couples of the surveyed families are clubbed into four categories of birth performance – the couples having the live birth at most 2, 3-4, 5-6, and 7 and above.

Applying F-test on the variation in the average family income due to the number of live births ever born to mothers, the relation was found insignificant at 5% level of significance (F=2.50, P>0.05) (Table–4.17). In other words, the income level does not significantly vary with couple's reproductive performance in the population. But, this inference is drawn without considering the joint effects of other factors under investigation. The significance might be due to the fact that just after delivery tribal women, particularly women in Chandel assume their normal works or duties. They do not care of health due to lack of health knowledge. The highest income level in the distribution say Rs. 14837 ± 16657 with 95% CI: 12102-17571 was observed in the families having number of live birth at most 2 while overall average family income of the population was Rs. 12244 ± 14830 with its 95% CI: 10799-13689. It was interestingly observed that excluding the first category there was a positive relation between number of live birth ever born and income. It may be explained in such a way that the pattern of variation in the income level with respect to number of children may perhaps be linked with agricultural income in the sense that major share of family income depend on agriculture production. Agricultural production in hilly region has mainly determined by number of family members or so called size of family.

Table–4.17

Differential monthly income according to fertility level

No. of live birth ever born	No. of house-holds (%)	Mean ± S.D	95%CI for mean	Test values
Up to 2	394 (36.8)	14837 ± 16657	12102-17571	F=2.50,
3-4	390 (36.4)	10467 ± 13921	8190-12744	P>0.05
5-6	217 (20.3)	10709 ± 13599	7663-13755	
7+	70 (6.5)	13556 ± 13237	8209-18902	
Total	**1071 (100)**	**12244 ± 14830**	**10799-13689**	

4.11 Family Income according to Child Mortality

Higher child mortality implies lower health condition and

frequent morbidity which would affect working hour and earning of family members on one hand and on the other, lower income would affect capital formation of the family which has another round of affect on the income. In this section, the surveyed couples have been categorized into three groups according the number of deceased child. About 7 percent of the total couples were found to have one child deceased in their live and 3 percent of families had at least two children deceased. The hypothesis of the present small section is that the child mortality affects not only reproductive indices but also the family income in the population. While overall average family income of the population was Rs. 12244 ± 14830 with its 95% CI: 10799-13689, the families having no deceased child were found to have their average family income of Rs. 12513 ± 15221 with its 95% CI: 10953-14074 (Table–4.18). The lower income of Rs. 11124 ± 11499 with 95% CI: 6576-15673 was observed in the families having one child deceased and it was alarmingly reduced to Rs. 6499 ± 5815 with 95% CI: 2804-10194 in the families which had experienced at least two children deceased. Irrespective of the effects of other variables, the income levels is visibly related with the number of deceased children in the family in this particular distribution. However, the variation in the income level is statistically insignificant according to number of deceased child in the population as evidenced by the value of F-statistics (1.04, P>0.05).

Table–4.18

Differential monthly income (in Rs.) according to the number of children born alive now deceased to a woman

No. of children	No. of house-holds (%)	Mean ± S.D	95%CI for mean	Test values
Nil	966 (90.2)	12513 ± 15221	10953-14074	F=1.04, P>0.05
One	71 (6.6)	11124 ± 11499	6576-15673	
At least 2	34 (3.2)	6499 ± 5815	2804-10194	
Total	**1071 (100)**	**12244 ± 14830**	**10799-13689**	

In short, various socio-economic variables, such as residence of households, sub-divisions, family systems, tribes, religions, family size, female family member, literacy rate, educational level, number of female members engaged in agriculture and allied activities, age at first marriage, age at first delivery, number of live birth, child mortality were taken up to see their relation with income in this chapter. Among these variables only six variables were significantly related to the variation in income. The significant variables were sub-divisions, size of female member, literacy rate, educational level, number of family member engaged in agriculture and live births. In the next section, multivariate analysis on correlates of income differentials is investigated.

4.12 Multivariate Analysis on the Correlates of Income Differentials

4.12.1 Introduction

The above sections show simply the association between income and other socio-economic variables. The present section discusses with the help of regression analysis. Regression analysis shows the relation between dependent variable (income) and explanatory variables (socio-economic variables). It is to estimate and/or predict the population means value of the dependent variable in terms of known or fixed values of explanatory variables obtained from the sampling. Though regression analysis does not necessarily mean causation, it reveals the precise causation on the basis of relation supported by the theory. So, the present study attempts to see the dependence of a variable, income on ten socio-economic variables which are hypothesized to have significant impact on income by using regression analysis.

4.12.2 Statistical Models

In recent years, many social scientists have tried to detect the important explanatory variables that affect income. The variation in the income of a family may be influenced by various families' background like social structure, source of income, infrastructures, socio-demographic factors etc. Generally, regression analysis is used for such study. In the situation where there are many explanatory variables, the model of multiple regression models. The general form of the multiple regression models is

$$\psi_i = \beta_0 + \beta_1 X_{1i} + \beta_2 X_{2i} + ... + \beta_K X_{Ki} + \varepsilon_i \qquad (1)$$

where k denotes the number of explanatory variables (X) and i denotes the ith family of the population concerned and β_i's are regression coefficients. The corresponding estimated model, pertaining to a particular sample from the population, is

$$Y_i = \beta_0 + \beta_1 X_{1i} + \beta_2 X_{2i} + ... + b_k X_{ki} + \varepsilon_i \qquad (2)$$

The equations (1) and (2) serve as a statistical model. However, we need to invoke again the assumptions of linearity, homoscedasticity, and independence. 'Linearity' means that the mean of the disturbances is zero at each combination of the predictor variables, that is $E(\varepsilon_i) = 0$ at every point (X_1, X_2, ..., X_k).'Homoscedasticity' means that the variance of ε is the same for each combination of the explanatory variables; that is, Var(ε_i) at every point (X_1, X_2, ... , X_k). 'Independence' again means that ε_i are statistically independent. Fitting the model involves minimizing the sum of squared residuals (least squares estimates) between estimated and observed values of the response variable, say amount of improvement in annual income per family. In general, if there are k-predictor variables, we must set k+1 partial derivatives equal to zero and solve k+1 equations for k+1 unknown regression parameters.

4.12.3 Multicollinearity

In fitting of regression models, two explanatory variables are said to have multicollinear if they are highly correlated. Thus, three or more predictor variables are multicollinear if at least one of them can be expressed as a close-fitting linear function of the others. In other words, the problem of multicollinearity is one of statistical instability of regression coefficients due to inadequate spread. So, we like to specify multiple regression models so that the predictor variables are not highly multicollinear. In most of the real-life observations, a certain amount of multicollinearity is inevitable as most of the predictor variables of interest are correlated to some extent. As a rough rule of thumb, when two predictor variables are correlated but both are relevant to the explanation from a theoretical point of view, we should not eliminate one of the variables to reduce multicollinearity, unless the correlations are higher in absolute magnitude than about 0.8 (Retherford, 1998). It means that we must live with a certain amount of multicollinearity. However, 0.35 is used to detect the problem in the sense that 0.35 is cut-off value of zero-order correlation coefficient in the present analysis.

4.12.4 Statistical Inference

We consider the regression coefficient 'b' from the estimated least square line. We can use b to make statements about β, the coefficient of X in the underlying population from which the sample is drawn. The first step is to consider the sampling distribution of b, which is the probability distribution of b over repeated samples from the same underlying population. The sampling distribution of b is derived theoretically, not by actually taking repeated samples. Normally only one real sample is available for analysis. However, statistical theory enables us to estimate the standard deviation of the sampling distribution of b. This standard deviation called standard error of b, is denoted by S_b. It can be calculated from the sample data and printed out, along with b itself, by standard computer programme (SPSS at present analysis) for linear regression. If a value of β is hypothesised and S_b has been calculated from the sample data, b may be transformed into t-statistic say,

$$t = \frac{b - \beta}{S_b} \qquad (3)$$

where t is the difference between b and β, measured in standard deviation units. The hypothesis according to which 'o' value is assigned to β is called null hypothesis. The reason why b is transformed to t is that t has a known sampling distribution (Student's-t distribution) with desirable statistical properties.

Precisely, it is to test if a random sample (x_i, y_i), i takes values from 1 to n has been drawn from a bivariate normal population in which regression coefficient of Y on X is β. The line of regression of Y on X (for the given sample) is

$$Y - \bar{y} = b\left(X - \bar{x}\right),\ b = \frac{\mu_{11}}{\sigma_x^2}$$

The estimate of Y for a given value x_i of X as given by the above line is

$$\hat{y}_i = \bar{y} + b\left(x_i - \bar{x}\right)$$

Under the null hypothesis that the population regression coefficient is β, then the statistic

$$t = \left(b - \beta\right)\left[\frac{(n-2)\sum_i \left(x_i - \bar{x}\right)^2}{\sum_i \left(y_i - \hat{y}\right)^2}\right]^{\frac{1}{2}}$$

follows t-distribution with (n-2) d.f. This is equivalent to (3).

4.12.5 Dummy Variable

Dummy variables were used to represent categorical variables such as place of residence (urban/rural), employment status (employed/unemployed) etc. It is also called dichotomous variables, binary variables, or contrast variables. Dummy variables take on only two values, usually 0 and 1 for two categories. Categorical variables with two categories can be represented by a single dummy variable. The variable - place of residence may be an example:

X: 1, urban (U) if the respondent resides in urban residence and
0, rural (R) if the respondent resides in rural residence.

The category with assigned value 0 is called the reference category. In this example, rural residence is the reference category. However, we might just as well have defined urban residence as the reference category:

X: 1, if the respondent residesin rural residence, 0 otherwise that is urban

Here, it makes no difference which category is chosen as the reference category. For instance, we regress 'per capita income of a family' (in thousand rupees) sayY on U:

$$\hat{y} = a + bU \quad (1)$$

Because, Y = 1- R, we can derive the regression of Y on U directly from (1) as

$$\hat{y} = a + b\,(1 - R) = (a + b) - bR = a^* - bR \quad (2)$$

4.12.6 Specification of Variables

In the present regression analysis, the response variable was considered to be the family monthly income (in rupee). The level of the family income was assumed to be functionally related with only ten explanatory factors of interest. They are place of residence (urban =1, rural =0); couple's educational level (levels: illiterate, literate but under matriculate, matriculate but under 10+2 standard, 10+2 standard but undergraduate and graduate and above); number of literate persons in the family; employment status (1 if any one of the family members is Govt. employee, 0 if non of any family members are Government employee); the area of cultivable land (in acre); number of family members engaged in agriculture and allied activities, type of family (nuclear and joint families). Under the caption of demographic variable, female age at marriage and number of live birth ever born to a woman were also included in the set of explanatory variables in the sense that such factors were assumed to be related with socio-economic development of a society.

4.12.7 Functional Relationship

In case of functional relationship, the family monthly

income of a family (Y) is defined to be a function of ten variables – area under rice cultivation, place of residence, type of family, number of family members engaged in agriculture and allied activities, number of literate persons in the family, educational status for both spouses, employment status, female age at marriage and number of live birth ever born to a married woman.

4.12.8 Hypothesis

The null hypothesis (H_0) of the present investigation may be spelt out as H_0: $\beta_i = 0$, each regression coefficient is zero indicating that the income of a family is not influenced by their socio-economic and demographic factors as against the alternative hypothesis (H_1), pronounced by H_1: $\beta_i \neq 0$, that is the income of a family is significantly influenced by the socio-economic and demographic factors of the family.

4.12.9 Results and Discussions

To quantify some qualitative variables, binary dummy variable (0, 1) technique was used and 0.35 was also taken as a cut off zero-order correlation value for scanning the multicollinearity problems among the explanatory variables. While interpreting the findings measuring the effects of the socio-economic factors on income levels, the regression coefficient (β) with its 95% confidence interval (CI) and P-values of the t-test for the coefficients were used. The probability levels of significance have been advocated by 5% ($P<0.05$), as statistical significance and 1% ($P<0.01$) as highly significant.

In the present analysis, the monthly income of family under observation was assumed to be functionally related with ten variables mentioned elsewhere. It was evident that the null hypothesis was rejected in the sense that all regression coefficients (β_i) can not be zero indicating that some of the explanatory variables had significant impacts on the income level. It was evidenced by F-value of the regression model, say 33.13 ($P<0.01$) (Table–4.19). The total variation in the family income was explained about 31% ($R^2=0.314$) by the explanatory variables or so called predictors. Out of ten variables five ones were observed to have their significant contributions on the variation of income level in the population. They were area under rice cultivation ($P<0.05$), number of family members engaged in agriculture and allied activities ($P<0.01$), number of literate persons in a family ($P<0.05$), educational level of male spouse ($P<0.01$) and number of live births ever born to a women ($P<0.05$). After adjusted the joint effects of other nine variables, area under rice cultivation has positive influence on the family's income in the sense that about rupees two hundred forty three could be enhanced in the annual income of a family with an increment of one acre of rice cultivation as quantified as b=243 (95% CI: 103-483, $P<0.05$).

Apart from the statistical significance, if one of the family members was government employed, the family monthly income would correspondingly be increased by Rs. 5316 (b=5316 with 95% CI: 197–10,829, $P>0.05$). This effect may be interpreted that government employment had somewhat influences on the advancement of family income, despite statistically insignificance. This insignificance might be due to limited numbers of government employees in the surveyed population under the study. Education had also been found to have its positive impact on the income level when controlled the joint effects of other variables. In this context, the income level of a family could be increased by Rs. 3764 per month when there is an advancement of one level in the education of male spouse. This improvement was highly significant ($P<0.01$) while adjusted the joint effects of other nine explanatory variables under study. Though having some visible improvement in the income level (Rs. 1822 per month), the educational level of female spouse had statistically insignificant impact on family income while controlling the joint effects of other nine variables including education of male spouse. This might also be due to limited number of female in educational levels and hence their income generation. But, the number of literate persons in the family was found to be positively associated with income level and highly significant ($P<0.01$).

Table–4.19
Multiple regression coefficients and their test values

Variables	β (95% CI)	t-value
(Constant)	4736 (2357, 11832)	3.424 (P<0.01)
Area under rice cultivation (in acre)*	243 (103, 483)	2.04 (P<0.05)
Place of residence	–3752 (–8183, 679)	1.665 (P>0.05)
Type of family	7431 (–765,15627)	1.78 (P>0.05)
No. of family members engaged in agricultural activities**	1259 (712, 2766)	3.37 (P<0.01)
Employment status of one of the family members	5316 (–197, 10829)	1.90 (P>0.05)
No. of literate persons in a family**	1259 (524, 1995)	3.37 (P<0.01)
Educational status of male spouse**	3764 (2289, 5240)	5.02 (P<0.01)
Educational status of female spouse	1822 (243, 3887)	1.74 (P>0.05)
Female age at marriage	–72 (–202, –57)	1.10 (P>0.05)
No. of live birth ever born to a women*	–818 (–1596, –39)	2.07 (P<0.05)

Model Diagnostics: F = 33.13 (P<0.01); R^2=0.314
* significant at 5% level of significance;
** significant at 1% level of significance

Family income was negatively associated (P<0.05) with the number of live births ever born to a woman (b=–818 with 95% CI: –1596, –39). In crude sense, it may be interpreted that the family income could not be improved because of higher fertility of the respondent. To each increment of one live birth, the corresponding family income would be reduced by Rs. 818 per month while controlled the effects of other nine predictors under investigation. This negative impact was statistically significant at 0.05 probability level of significance. The fitted multiple regression models on the family income (Y in rupees per month) may be expressed as:

Y = 4736 + 243 (area under rice cultivation) – 3752(place of residence) + 7431 (type of family) + 1733(number of family members engaged in rice cultivation) + 5316 (employment status) + 1259 (number of literate persons in the family) + 3764 (education of male spouse) + 1822 (education of female spouse) – 72 (female age at marriage) – 818 (number of live birth to a woman)

In the present investigation, the five predictors – education particularly of male spouse, number of literate persons in the family, number of family member engaged in rice cultivation, area under rice cultivation and number of live birth ever born to a woman could be identified as main determinants of the income differential of the people of Chandel District in Manipur (India). The significant positive association between educational level and economic status is in agreement with the similar views of Tungdin and Kapoor (2010) and Puttaraja and Heggade (2012). Also, the views of larger cultivable land enhances the economic status of the people is supported by the findings of Dewangan et al., (2011) because almost all households depend on agriculture and allied activities for their livelihood. Thus, policy makers should give priority on the enhancement of educational level of tribal people, development of agriculture and allied sector and control of fertility for development and welfare of tribal people in general and Chandel district in particular.

5

Chapter

Impact of Socio-Economic Variables on Rice Production

5.1 Introduction

As in most of the rural areas of India, agriculture is the dominant occupation of the people of Manipur. It is not only the main source of livelihood of the overwhelming majority, but also a tradition and a way of life that moulds the socio-economic status of the people. According to 2011 census, more than half (52%) of the total working population of the state were directly dependent on agriculture for their livelihood. Out of the total working population of 11,59,053 persons, 2,66,486 persons (23%) in the valley and 3,02,466 persons (26%) in the hill were agricultural workers. A large number of populations in the state pursue agriculture as secondary occupation, even though agriculture is not their primary occupation. Agriculture provides almost all the entire food requirements of the people in the state in one sense and it also provides raw materials for a limited agro-based industries. The nature of agriculture in hill areas differs from that of valley due to differences in physical configuration, climatic pattern, soil fertility and differential applicability technological and scientific development.

In contrast with types of cultivation in valley districts, shifting/jhum cultivation and terrace farming are practiced in hill slopes bringing limited subsistence production. Performance of agriculture in the state mainly depends on natural supports, viz. timely rainfall and weather conditions. Rice is the staple food and is grown in hill and plain areas and it accounted for about 97.46% of the total food grains production of the state in 2012-13. The production of rice in 2014-15 was estimated at 482.25 thousand tonnes which was more than the preceding year's rice output of 477.05 thousand tonnes. In case of maize, the second major cereal crop in the state production in 2014-15 was estimated to be 11.32 thousand tonnes as against 11.55 thousand tonnes in the preceding year (Government of Manipur, 2017)[10]. Agriculture being the main contributing sector to the state income, say Net State Domestic Product (NSDP), any variation in the production of rice has a direct impact on the income and welfare of the people who depend on it. Despite being the leading sector in the state, some signs of the traditional agriculture, which we have inherited from ancestors, are still woven around this sector in the realm of many years of economic planning. But during these years, the Government of Manipur has taken up development programmes to increase agricultural production in the hills and valley through innovations and modernization of the agricultural practices.

In Chandel district about 50% of total gross cropped area was under rice cultivation in 2014-15. Among the hill district, yield of rice (kg/ hec.) was also highest in the district (3410.26) which was followed by that in Ukhrul (2540.04). This yield figure was also above the state figure (2706.23) in the same year. In the context of above scenario this chapter examines the impact of socio-economic factors on rice production in the district.

5.2 Specification of Variables

In the present analysis, the response dependent variable considered is agriculture production as quantified by the "production of rice (in kg)". The variation in the response variable is assumed to be functionally related with eleven independent variables. The analysis is performed for both wet land and the shifting cultivation. The independent

10. Government of Manipur (2017) : Economic Survey Manipur 2016-17, P. 54. Directorate of Economics and Statistics.

(explanatory) variables/predictors under wet cultivation are area under rice cultivation (in acre), number of male engaged in rice cultivation, number of female engaged in rice cultivation, labour cost (in '00 Re.), cost of fertilizer (in '00Re.), cost of pesticide (in '00 Re.), cost of insecticide (in '00 Re.), cost of bullock/tractor (in '00 Re.), irrigation facility (Yes=1 & No=0), number of literate persons in the family, and total number family members in a household. Under shifting cultivation, the independent variables are area under rice cultivation (in acre), number of male engaged in rice cultivation, number of female engaged in rice cultivation, labour cost (in '00 Re.), number of literate persons in the family, Jhum cycle (in year) and size of family as defined by the total number family members in a household under survey.

5.3 Functional Relationship

In this multiple regression model, the quantity of rice production (Y) is assumed to be functionally related with twelve factors (X_i; i=1, 2, 3, ..., 12) in Chandel district of Manipur. It may be expressed as $Y=f(X_1, X_2, X_3, ..., X_{12})$. Precisely,

Quantity of the production of rice under Wet-Cultivation = f(area under rice cultivation, number of male labour, number of female labour, labour cost, cost of fertilizer, cost of pesticide, cost of insecticide, cost of bullock/tractor, irrigation facility, number of literate family member, and family size).

Quantity of the production of rice under Shifting-Cultivation= f(area under rice cultivation, number of male labour, number of female labour, labour cost, jhum cycle, number of literate family member, and family size).

5.4 Hypothesis in the Models

The null hypothesis (H_0) of the present analysis is given by

H0: $\beta_i=0$, (each regression coefficient is zero). In other words, the quantity of the rice production is not influenced by the explanatory/independent variables as against the alternative hypothesis (H_1), defined by

H1: $\beta_i \neq 0$, the rice production is significantly influenced by the explanatory variables.

5.5 Analysis

For each cultivation type – wet (281 households) and shifting (308 households), the present multiple regression analysis was being performed for Chandel district as a whole and 4 sub-divisions (Machi, Tengnoupal, Chakpikarong and Chandel). In the sub-division wise analysis, the step wise regressions models were also developed. Using the zero order correlation matrix, the problem of multicollinearity was scanned and controlled at $r = 0.50$. The results of the analysis were interpreted in term of regression coefficients, t-value with 95% confidence interval (CI) and P-value. The regression coefficients (β_i) were computed by utilizing both quantitative and categorical variables. Under categorical variable, the irrigation facility is defined by a binary dummy variable for easier way of interpretation. It was defined by 1 (one) when the cultivated field under rice had irrigation facility and by 0 (zero) when the field had no such facility. From the regression diagnostics, the model was evident that the null hypothesis was rejected in the sense that all the regression coefficients (β_i) of the predictors can not be zero. Some of the explanatory variables had significant impacts on the quantity of the rice production in the population under study. It was evidenced by F-value of the regression model, say 6.23 ($P<0.001$) (Table–5.1).

Table–5.1
Multiple regression coefficients (b) and their significance level under wet-cultivation in Chandel district

Explanatory variables	B	S.E	t	P	95%CI for B Lower	95%CI for B Upper
(Constant)**	1822.66	273.33	6.67	0.000	1284.53	2360.80
Area under rice cultivation (in acre)**	–235.99	71.26	-3.31	0.001	-376.29	-95.70
Number of male labour	–28.99	58.24	–0.50	0.619	–143.66	85.68
Number of female labour	23.80	61.89	0.38	0.701	–98.06	145.66
No. of literate persons in the family	–36.23	27.15	–1.34	0.183	–89.68	17.22
Irrigation facility**	794.96	121.34	6.55	0.000	556.06	1033.86
Labour cost (in '00Rs.)	1.73	2.30	0.75	0.454	–2.80	6.26
Cost of fertilizer (in '00Rs.)	0.09	2.96	0.03	0.976	–5.74	5.92
Cost of pesticide (in '00Rs.)	8.85	78.96	0.11	0.911	–146.62	164.31
Cost of insecticide (in '00Rs.)	1.88	29.91	0.06	0.950	–57.01	60.77
Cost of bullock/ tractor (in '00Rs.)	–3.37	6.96	–0.49	0.628	–17.07	10.32
Size of family	–26.06	29.43	–0.89	0.377	–84.00	31.89

Model Diagnostics: $F_{(11,269)} = 6.23$, $P<0.001$;
$R^2 = 0.32$, Durbin Watson = 1.965
* significant at 0.05 probability level
** significant at 0.01 probability level

In this multiple regression model, the rice production was found to be 1823 kg per acre when there were no effects of the explanatory variables under study. Only two predictors out of the eleven background variables were confirmed to have high significant contribution on the variation in the rice production under wet cultivation system. After adjusted the joint effects of the combination of ten other explanatory variables, the two variables say area under rice cultivation

($P<0.01$) and irrigation facility ($P<0.01$) had significant impact on the quantity of rice production (Table–5.1.)

To each increment of one acre, the rice production was significantly decreased about 236 kg if the joint effects of other ten variables were controlled at their central level. It was evidenced by regression coefficient (b=–235.99 and standard error, (S. E) of 71.26) with 95% CI: [(–376.29) – (–95.70)], absolute value of 't' (t=3.31) which was highly significant at 1% probability level of significance ($P<0.01$). The negative value of area was contradictory to common sense and logical argument. Further study is required to explain why it has negative sign. However, it might also be due to negligence of the farmers who extend the area of cultivation under his control. Moreover, it implies that it is increasingly difficult to cultivate rice cultivation in hill slope with larger size of holdings. Though statistically insignificant, the quantity of rice production was shown to be increased according to increased number of female labour after controlling the joint effects of other explanatory variables under consideration as witnessed by test value and b=23.80 (with 95% CI: –98.06–145.66). When controlled the joint effects of other variables – area under rice cultivation, number of male labour, number of female labour, labour cost, cost of fertilizer, cost of pesticide, cost of insecticide, cost of bullock/tractor, number of literate family member, and family size, the irrigation facility was observed to have high significant impact on rice production in the population. The present finding may be interpreted as the quantity of the rice production was increased by 795 kg per acre in the field having irrigation system than that of no irrigation system. This improvement in rice production could be obtained when the joint effects of other variables are keeping constant at their average level. It was statistically evident with b(=794.96 with 95% CI: 556.06–1033.86) and (t=6.55; $P<0.01$). It is also interesting to note that cost of modern inputs such as cost of fertilizers, pesticides and insecticides were insignificant at 5%. This shows that they don't bother about the prices of these inputs. They buy according to their needs ignoring the price levels of these inputs.

The developed model for study population (Chandel district) was given by

> Quantity of the production of rice under Wet-Cultivation = 1822.66 – 235.99 (area under rice cultivation) – 28.99 (No. of male labour) + 23.80 (No. of female labour) + 1.73 (labour cost) + 0.09 (cost of fertilizer) + 8.85 (cost of pesticide) + 1.88 (cost of insecticide) – 3.37 (cost of bullock/tractor) + 794.96 (irrigation facility) – 36.23 (No. of literate family member) – 26.06 (size of family).

5.5.1 Models of Sub-Divisions under Wet-Cultivation

The multiple regression analysis was further performed for four sub-divisions – Machi, Tengnoupal, Chandel and Chakpikarong. While only two factors out of the eleven ones were observed to have significant impact on the quantity of the production of rice under Wet-Cultivation in the Chandel district, in Machi sub-division, three independent variables - area under rice cultivation ($P<0.01$), irrigation facility ($P<0.01$) and cost of fertilizer ($P<0.01$) significantly influenced on the rice production. The regression model so developed from the Machi sub-division highlighted that expected mean value of rice production was 2200 kg per acre of agriculture (Wet) land when the joint effects of all ten predictors was keeping constant. In this sub-division to each increment of one acre of land under rice cultivation, the rice production would significantly be reduced by 321 kg while keeping constant the joint effect of other nine independent variables – number of male labour, number of female labour, labour cost, cost of fertilizer, cost of pesticide, cost of insecticide, irrigation facility, number of literate family member, and family size. It was shown by the test (t) value, 3.14 ($P<0.01$) for the regression coefficient b (–321) with 95% CI: –524.92 to –17.05. The other two significant variables were irrigation facility ($b=507$ with 95% CI: 128.62–885.55) as revealed by the test value, ($t=2.67$, $P<0.01$) and cost of fertilizer ($b=21.71$ with 95% CI: 7.67–35.75) and its t-value, 3.08 ($P<0.01$) while keeping constant the joint effect of other predictors. The sign of literate family member was negative that is production declines when number literate increases.

This contradictory to common believe (Table–5.2). The decline in rice production in response to the increase in the number of literate labour might be explained by changing work culture of the farmers in a traditional society. When they become literate they have an ego of superiority and are unwilling to work. In other words as farmers become literate or more educated, they are willing to less work. The developed model wasalso found to be significant as supported by the diagnostics, F=4.87 (P<0.01), R2=0.34 and the value of Durbin-Watson (D) statistic, 1.93 which is approaching to 2.

Thus, the regression models developed for Machi sub-division was given by

Quantity of the rice production under wet-cultivation in Machi sub-division = 2199.98 – 320.98 (area under rice cultivation) – 1.98 (No. of male labour) – 136.13 (No. of female labour) – 0.53 (labour cost) + 21.71(cost of fertilizer) – 120.96 (cost of pesticide) + 25.90 (cost of insecticide) + 507.08 (irrigation facility) – 58.56 (No. of literate family member) – 56.81(size of family) with model diagnostics: F=4.87 (P<0.01), R^2=0.34, D=1.93.

Regression model developed from the Tengnoupal sub-division observed that the expected mean value of rice cultivation was 1253 kg per acre of land under rice cultivation when the joint effect of other ten independent variables was constant. Apart from the pattern of Machi sub-division, only one variable say irrigation facility was found to be significant. It was quantified by regression coefficient, b (1596.11 with 95% CI: 506.10–1185.74) and t-value, 4.94 (P<0.01). Here, it is interpreted that the rice production was increased by 1596 kg per acre when there is an increase of one acre of irrigated area under rice cultivation. It was obtained when the joint effect of other nine independent variables remained the same.

Table–5.2
Regression coefficients (b) and their significance levelunder wet-cultivation in Machi sub-division

Explanatory variables	b	S.E	t	P	95%CI for B Lower	Upper
(Constant)**	2199.98	343.87	6.40	0.000	1515.11	2884.85
Area under rice cultivation (in acre)**	–320.98	102.40	–3.14	0.002	–524.92	–17.05
No. of male labour	–1.98	87.26	–0.02	0.982	–175.79	171.82
No. of female labour	–136.13	92.20	–1.48	0.144	–319.77	47.51
No. of literate family member	–58.56	42.48	–1.38	0.172	–143.17	26.05
Irrigation facility**	507.08	190.02	2.67	0.009	128.62	885.55
Cost of fertilizer (in '00Rs.)**	21.71	7.05	3.08	0.003	7.67	35.75
Cost of pesticide (in '00Rs.)	–120.96	106.81	–1.13	0.261	–333.69	91.76
Cost of insecticide (in '00Rs.)	25.90	25.09	1.03	0.305	–24.07	75.87
Size of family	–56.81	49.08	–1.16	0.251	–154.56	40.94
Labour cost (in '00Rs.)	–0.53	4.66	–0.11	0.910	–9.82	8.76

* significant at 0.05 probability level;

** significant at 0.01 probability level

Table–5.3
Regression coefficients (b) and their significance level under wet-cultivation in Tengnoupal sub-division

Explanatory variables	b	S.E	t	P	95%CI for B Lower	Upper
Constant	1252.77	1318.43	0.95	0.350	–452.43	3957.97
Area of agriculture land (in acre)	–187.29	315.31	–0.59	0.557	–834.24	459.66
No. of male labour	54.61	327.69	0.17	0.869	–617.75	726.97
No. of female labour	372.39	369.83	1.01	0.323	–386.43	1131.21
No. of literate family member	–203.97	139.03	–1.47	0.154	–489.23	81.30
Irrigation facility**	1596.11	490.37	3.26	0.003	589.97	2602.26

Cost of fertilizer (in '00Rs.)	8.18	23.39	0.35	0.729	–39.82	56.18
Cost of pesticide (in '00Rs.)	56.57	450.79	0.13	0.901	–868.38	981.51
Cost of insecticide (in '00Rs.)	–181.91	447.47	–0.41	0.688	–110.04	736.22
Size of family	–49.52	117.66	–0.42	0.677	–290.93	191.89
Labour cost (in '00Rs.)	–3.85	9.34	–0.41	0.683	–23.02	15.31

* significant at 0.05 probability level;

** significant at 0.01 probability level

The obtained model was also found to be significant, as witnessed by the diagnostics, F=3.64 ($P<0.01$), $R^2=0.38$ and the value of Durbin-Watson (D) statistic, 1.97 tending to 2 (Table–5.3). The fitted model also suggests that the ten independent variables of interest explained 38 percent of the total variation in the rice production of the Tengnoupal sub-division in Chandel district under wet cultivation system.

Here, the regression models developed for Tengnoupal sub-division was given by

> Quantity of the rice production under wet-cultivation in Tengnoupal sub-division = 1252.77–187.29 (area under rice cultivation) + 54.61 (No. of male labour) + 372.39 (No. of female labour) – 3.85 (labour cost) + 8.18 (cost of fertilizer) + 56.57 (cost of pesticide) – 181.91 (cost of insecticide) + 1596.11 (irrigation facility) – 203.97 (No. literate family member) – 49.52 (size of family) with model diagnostics: F=3.64 ($P<0.01$), R2=0.38, D=1.97

The regression analysis was also run for Chandel sub-division, one of the clusters of the population with particular reference to wet-cultivation. Out of 10 regression coefficients, only two regression coefficients that is coefficient for irrigation and labour cost were significant at 1 percent and 5 percent respectively. Regression coefficient of irrigation shows rice production would increase by 846 kg per acre when irrigated area of one acre increases. The coefficient of labour cost was positive which is contrary to expectation. Further research is call for to examine the sign of labour cost. However, this increase in production as indicated by the positive sign might be due to increase in consciousness of farmers in term of timely application of labour hour and substitution of labour by other factors of production including area under irrigation. Another explanation of this result might be the substitution of using insecticides and weedicides for labour when the cost of labour increase. This relation between cost of labour and rice production may also be explained in terms of substitution between higher labour and family own labour. When cost of labour increase, agriculture families became conscious and try to substitute for hired labour. Since they work their own farms they are more efficient and hence increase the production. This model of Chandel sub-division highlighted that the expected mean rice output was 1423 kg per acre of agriculture (Wet) land when the joint effects of other ten predictors was constant. This regression was significant at one percent as shown by F-value (4.98). The regression models developed for Chandel sub-division was given by

Quantity of the rice production under wet-cultivation in Chandel sub-division = 1422.62 – 97.67 (area under rice cultivation) + 28.60 (No. of male labour) – 59.25 (No. of female labour) + 5.13 (labour cost) – 3.40 (cost of fertilizer) – 42.95 (cost of pesticide) + 5.11 (cost of insecticide) + 845.92 (irrigation facility) + 11.34 (No. of literate family member) – 46.02 (size of family) with model diagnostics: $F=4.98$ ($P<0.01$), $R^2=0.29$, $D=1.98$.

Table–5.4
Regression coefficients (b) and their significance level under wet-cultivation in Chandel sub-division

Explanatory variables	b	S.E	t	P	95%CI for B Lower	Upper
(Constant)**	1422.62	325.75	4.37	0.000	776.26	2068.98
Area of agriculture land (in acre)	–97.67	111.35	–0.88	0.383	–318.62	123.28
No. of male labour	28.60	72.93	0.39	0.696	–116.11	173.31

No. of female labour	–59.25	78.39	–0.76	0.452	–214.79	96.29
No. of literate family member	11.34	33.24	0.34	0.734	–54.61	77.30
Irrigation facility**	845.92	171.26	4.94	0.000	506.10	1185.74
Cost of fertilizer (in '00Rs.)	–3.40	2.74	–1.24	0.216	–8.83	2.03
Cost of pesticide (in '00Rs.)	–42.95	148.96	–0.29	0.774	–338.53	252.62
Cost of insecticide (in '00Rs.)	5.11	191.04	0.03	0.979	–373.95	384.17
Size of family	–46.02	37.47	–1.23	0.222	–120.37	28.33
Labour cost (in '00Rs.)*	5.13	2.50	2.06	0.042	0.18	10.09

* significant at 0.05 probability level;
** significant at 0.01 probability level

As in the case of Machi sub-division, only two factors out of the ten independent variables were observed to have significant impacts on the quantity of rice production under wet-cultivation system in Chandel sub-division. The two variables were irrigation facility ($P<0.01$) and labour cost ($P<0.05$). When controlled the joint effects of the nine predictors – area under rice cultivation, number of male labour, number of female labour, cost of fertilizer, cost of pesticide, cost of insecticide, number of literate family member, labour cost, and family size; the rice production significantly increased by 846 kg (with 95% CI: 506.10–1185.74) for every addition of one acre having good irrigation facility. It was witnessed by test value ($t=4.94$, $P<0.01$). The value of the test statistic, 2.1 ($P<0.05$) suggested that the rice production was observed to be significantly increased by 5kg per acre (with 95%CI: 0.18–10.09) to each increment of Rs. 100 in labour cost while keeping constant the effects of other variables. Though having only two statistically significant predictors, the fitted model was found to be significant as evidenced by the model diagnostics, $F=4.87$ ($P<0.01$), $D=1.98$ and $R^2=0.34$. The value of R^2 highlighted the ten independent variables explained 34% of the total variation in the rice production of the Chandel sub-division in the population under study.

Table–5.5
Regression coefficients (b) and their significance levelunderwet-cultivation in Chakpikarong sub-division

Explanatory variables	b	S.E	t	P	95%CI for B Lower	95%CI for B Upper
(Constant)*	1400.14	744.43	1.88	0.038	–111.14	2911.42
Area under rice cultivation (in acre)	–439.24	234.56	–1.87	0.069	–915.42	36.95
No. of male labour	–168.58	181.22	–0.93	0.359	–536.49	199.32
No. of female labour*	380.29	185.90	2.05	0.048	92.89	757.69
No. of literate family member	43.47	93.14	0.47	0.644	–145.61	232.54
Irrigation facility*	818.39	360.78	2.27	0.030	85.97	1550.81
Cost of fertilizer (in '00Rs.)	–4.13	14.71	–0.28	0.781	–33.98	25.73
Cost of pesticide (in '00Rs.)	–176.68	433.83	–0.41	0.686	–1057.41	704.05
Cost of insecticide (in '00Rs.)	516.59	532.24	0.97	0.338	–563.91	1597.09
Size of family	21.08	94.24	0.22	0.824	–170.24	212.39
Labour cost (in '00Rs.)	–5.94	8.86	–0.67	0.507	–23.91	12.04

* significant at 0.05 probability level;
** significant at 0.01 probability level

In Chakpikarong sub-division, the fitted regression model was again highly significant as witnessed by its model diagnostics, F=3.62 ($P<0.01$), $R^2=0.32$ and D=2.03 (approaching to 2) (Table–5.5). This model with the ten independent variables explained 32% of the total variation in the rice production of this sub-division. Out of the ten independent variables, only two variables – number of female labour ($P<0.05$) and irrigation facility ($P<0.05$) had significant effects on the agriculture production (rice) while controlled the joint effects of other independent variables at their central level. Here, the expected value of rice production might be increased by 380 kg for each increase in one female labour in rice cultivation (with 95% CI: 92.89–757.69) with its standard error of 185.9 and the effects of other independent variables of interest were controlled.

The agricultural production could be increased by 818 kg (with 95% CI: 85.97–1550.81) when one acre of wet-land having irrigation facility increased while keeping constant the joint effects of the other nine variables under study. Hence, the regression models developed for Chakpikarong sub-division was given by

Quantity of the rice production under wet-cultivation in Chakpikarong sub-division = 1400.14–439.24 (area under rice cultivation) – 168.58 (No. of male labour) + 380.29 (No. of female labour) – 5.94 (labour cost) – 4.13 (cost of fertilizer) – 176.68 (cost of pesticide) + 516.59 (cost of insecticide) + 818.39 (irrigation facility) + 43.47 (No. of literate family member) + 21.08 (size of family) with model diagnostics: $F=3.62$ $(P<0.01)$, $R^2=0.32$, $D=2.03$.

5.5.2 Stepwise Models under Wet-Cultivation

In this regression analysis, step-wise method was applied to identify the more influencing variables on the variation in the rice production particularly in sub-divisions, namely Machi, Tengnoupal, Chandel and Chakpikarong in isolation. As in the previous case ten independent variables were included in the analysis. They were area under rice cultivation, number of male labour, number of female labour, cost of fertilizer, cost of pesticide, cost of insecticide, irrigation facility, number of literate family member, cost of bullock/tractor and family size.In Machi sub-division, the last model could be achieved in third model/step. The most influencing variables in the sub-division were irrigation facility, area under rice cultivation and cost of fertilizer. In the last fitted model, the expected mean value of production was 1533 kg per acre (with 95% CI: 1089.41–1976.62) when the effects of three predictors

Table–5.6

Stepwise regression coefficients (b) and their significance level under wet-cultivation in four sub-divisions of Chandel district

Sub-Division	Model	Explanatory variables	b	S.E	t	P	95%CI for B Lower	95%CI for B Upper
Machi	1	(Constant)**	1202.26	174.92	6.87	0.000	854.47	1550.06
		Irrigation facility**	596.47	195.01	3.06	0.003	208.74	984.21
	2	(Constant)**	1630.99	234.41	6.96	0.000	1164.83	2097.15
		Irrigation facility**	535.11	189.93	2.82	0.006	157.42	912.80
		Area under rice cultivation*	–221.80	83.99	–2.64	0.010	–388.84	–54.77
	3	(Constant)**	1533.01	223.03	6.87	0.000	1089.41	1976.62
		Irrigation facility*	452.51	180.83	2.50	0.014	92.83	812.18
		Area under rice cultivation**	–373.05	91.03	–4.10	0.000	–554.11	–191.99
		Cost of fertilizer (in '00Rs.)**	22.38	6.63	3.38	0.001	9.19	35.56
Tengnoupal	1	(Constant)*	837.57	343.73	2.44	0.020	140.45	1534.68
		Irrigation facility **	1458.73	415.55	3.51	0.000	615.96	2301.50
Chandel	1	(Constant)**	1119.54	149.21	7.50	0.000	823.79	1415.29
		Irrigation facility**	835.27	164.96	5.06	0.000	508.30	1162.24
	2	(Constant)**	958.87	158.02	6.07	0.000	645.61	1272.14
		Irrigation facility**	886.48	161.95	5.47	0.000	565.44	1207.52
		Labour cost (in '00Rs.)*	6.15	2.37	2.60	0.011	1.45	10.85

Sub-Division	Model	Explanatory variables	b	S.E	t	P	95%CI for B	
							Lower	Upper
Chakpikarong	1	(Constant)**	1434.45	282.47	5.08	0.000	865.17	2003.72
		Irrigation facility*	789.04	338.67	2.33	0.024	106.51	1471.58
	2	(Constant)*	863.25	381.76	2.26	0.029	93.36	1633.15
		Irrigation facility*	760.48	326.09	2.33	0.024	102.85	1418.11
		No. of female labour*	319.87	150.15	2.13	0.039	17.06	622.68

*significant at 0.05 probability level; **significant at 0.01 probability level

were controlled. The best model in the present analysis of the sub-division was given by the rice production is equal to 1533.01 + 452.51 (irrigation facility) – 373.05 (area of agriculture land) + 22.38 (cost of fertilizer). The model interprets that the rice production was increased by 453 kg per acre (95% CI: 92.83–812.18) with standard error of 181 kg of the land having good irrigation facility while the joint effect of two variables – area of agriculture land and cost of fertilizer are adjusted. It was statistically significant as evidenced by the test value, 2.5 ($P<0.05$).

In this last model, to each increment of one acre of agriculture land, the rice production might be reduced by 373 kg per acre (95% CI: –554 to –192) when adjusted the joint effect of two variables viz., irrigation facility and cost of fertilizer. Controlling the effects of irrigation facility and area of agriculture land, the rice production increased by 22.38 kg per acre for every increase of rupee one hundred in fertilizer price (with 95% CI: 9.14–35.56) which was highly significant ($t=3.38$, $P<0.01$). The fitted model of Machi sub-division was highly significant ($F=10.16$, $P<0.01$ and $D=1.83$). The significant three variables explained 27% of the total variation in the rice production in the sub-division as witnessed by the R^2 value (=0.269) which was gradually increased from 0.099 ($F=9.36$, $P<0.01$) and 0.168 ($F=8.49$, $P<0.01$) (Table–5.6 and Table–5.7). But, in Tengnoupal sub-division only one predictor say irrigation facility was observed to be significant as witnessed by the regression coefficient, 1458.73 with 95% CI: 615.95–2301.50 ($t=3.51$, $P<0.01$). It may be interestingly noted that only irrigation facility could explain 26% of the total variation in the rice production (Table–5.6 and Table–5.7).

Table–5.7

Model Summary of Stepwise regression analysis according to Sub-Division under wet-cultivation

Sub-division	Model	R^2	Adjusted R^2	Durbin Watson (D)	F-value	P-value
Machi	1	0.099	0.089		9.36	<0.01

	2	0.168	0.148		8.49	<0.01
	3	0.269	0.242	1.83	10.16	<0.01
Tengnoupal	1	0.255	0.234	1.92	12.32	<0.01
Chandel	1	0.192	0.184		25.64	<0.01
	2	0.240	0.226	1.72	16.87	<0.01
Chakpikarong	1	0.110	0.090		5.43	<0.05
	2	0.195	0.157	2.09	5.20	<0.01

In the second best model in Chandel sub-division, only two predictors say irrigation facility (P<0.01) and labour cost (P<0.05) were observed to be most influencing ones on the variation in rice production in the sub-population (Table–5.6) . In this fitted model, the expected mean value of rice production 959 kg per acre (95% CI: 646–1272) while adjusted the joint effect of the variables. The best model for the Chandel sub-division was given by the rice production was equal to 958.89 + 886.48 (irrigation facility) + 6.15 (labour cost). The model highlighted that the rice production was increased by 886.48 kg per acre of irrigated land (95%CI: 565.44–1207.52) with standard error of 161.95 while the effect of the cost of labour was controlled which was highly significant as witnessed by the t-value, 5.47 (P<0.01). Besides, the rice production increased by 6.15 kg (95% CI: 1.45–10.85) per acre to each increment of rupees one hundred of labour cost when adjusted the effect of irrigation facility in the sub-division. The last fitted model of Chandel sub-division was highly significant (F=16.87, P<0.01 and D=1.72) and the two variables explained 24% of the total variation in the rice production in the sub-division as witnessed by the R2 value (=0.240) which was increased from 0.192 (F=25.64, P<0.01) (Table–5.7).

The fitted model of the Chakpikarong sub-division was given by the rice production was equal to 863.23 + 760.48 (irrigation facility) + 319.87 (number of female labour) (Table–5.6). The model indicated that the rice production was increased by 760.48 kg per acre (95% CI: 102.85–1418.11) with standard error of 326.09 kg when one acre of land having irrigation facility was increased. This effect of irrigation facility was statistically significant, evidenced by the t-value, 2.33 ($P<0.05$). The rice production was increased by 319.87 kg (95%CI: 17.06–622.68) per acre to each increment of number of female labour engaged in the agriculture activities after adjusted the effect of irrigation facility in the Chakpikarong sub-division. The best model of Chakpikarong sub-division was highly significant ($F=5.20$, $P<0.01$ and $D=2.09$) and the two variables – irrigation facility and number of female labour engaged in the agriculture activities explain 20% of the total variation in the rice production as evidenced by the R^2 value (=0.195) which was increased from 0.110 ($F=5.43$, $P<0.05$) shown in Table–5.7.

5.6.1 Models under Shifting-Cultivation

In this analysis only seven independent variables were included in these models. The variables of interest were area under rice cultivation (in acre), Jhum cycle (in year), number of male labour engaged in agriculture activities, number of female labour engaged in rice cultivation (in acre), labour cost (in Rs. '00), number of literate persons in the family and size of family which was defined by the total number family members in a household under survey. Here, the rice production was found to be –313 kg per acre when there were no effects of the explanatory variables under study (Table–5.8). It indirectly indicated that the yield of shifting cultivation was solely depended on the independent variables under consideration. However, only three predictors out of the seven background variables were found to have their significant contributions on the variation in the rice production under shifting-cultivation system. When controlled the joint effects of the six other variables, each three variables say area under rice cultivation ($P<0.01$), Jhum cycle ($P<0.01$) and labour cost ($P<0.05$) were observed to have their significant impacts on the quantity of rice production in Chandel district.

For each increment of one acre, the rice production was significantly reduced by about 353 kg while the joint effects of other six independent variables were controlled. The regression coefficient of jhum cycle (b=136) was significant as shown by the statistical value of "t". It implies that the quantity of rice production might be increased according to increase in the number of jhum cycle after adjusted the joint effects of other explanatory variables namely, area of agriculture land (in acre), number of male labour engaged in agriculture activities, number of female labour engaged in agriculture activities, labour cost (in '00 Rs.), number of literate persons in the family and size of family.

Table–5.8
Multiple regression coefficients (b) and their significance level under shifting cultivation in Chandel district

Explanatory variables	b	S.E	t	P	95%CI for B Lower	95%CI for B Upper
(Constant)	–313.18	254.71	–1.23	0.220	–814.42	188.06
Area under rice cultivation (in acre)**	–352.80	61.27	–5.76	0.000	–473.38	–232.23
Jhum cycle (in yr)**	136.07	16.29	8.35	0.000	103.99	168.14
Size of family	30.61	27.69	1.11	0.270	–23.89	85.11
No. of male labour	–8.58	60.56	–0.14	0.887	–127.75	110.60
No. of female labour	–10.89	56.96	–0.19	0.848	–122.99	101.19
Labour cost (in '00Rs.)*	5.46	2.49	2.19	0.029	0.55	10.37
No. of literate family member	15.19	25.19	0.60	0.547	–34.37	64.77

Model Diagnostics: $F_{(7, 300)} = 13.64$, $P<0.001$;
$R^2 = 0.24$, Durbin Watson = 1.84
* significant at 0.05 probability level;
** significant at 0.01 probability level

This is due to the fact that increase in jhum cycle implies land left uncultivated longer period of time and hence fertile. Apart from statistically significance, the quantity of rice production may also be increased by 31 kg per acre to each increment of size of the family controlling the joint effects of other explanatory variables under consideration. It may perhaps be caused by the fact that size of family be associated with number of family members engaged with the agriculture activities in the population. While adjusted the joint effects of six other variables, the rice production was again observed to be significantly increased with the increase of labour cost. It is revealed by the coefficient of 5.46±2.49 kg with 95% CI of 0.55–10.37. It may be interpreted that to each increment of rupees one hundred in the labour cost, the rice production would be increased by 6 kg per acre which was statistically significant ($P<0.05$) after controlling the effects of other factors under study.

5.6.2 Models for Sub-Divisions under Shifting-Cultivation

The analysis is again done for shifting-cultivation in four sub-divisions – Machi, Tengnoupal, Chandel and Chakpikarong. Only four predictors were found to be significant influencing on rice production in Machi sub-division (Table–5.9). These variables were area under rice cultivation ($P<0.05$), jhum cycle ($P<0.01$), number of female labour ($P<0.01$) and labour cost ($P<0.01$). Area under rice cultivation was significant as evidenced by the absolute test (t) value, 2.54 ($P<0.05$) for the regression coefficient b (–371.47) with 95% CI: –664.16 to –78.79. The other three significant variables were jhum cycle (b=191.21 with 95% CI: 113.09–269.32) as witnessed by the test value, ($t=2.90$, $P<0.01$), number of female labour engaged in the rice cultivation (b=–405.18 with 95% CI: –749.14 to –61.21) and labour cost (b=27.97 with 95% CI: 9.27–46.67) while keeping constant the joint effect of other predictors in the Machi sub-division. The fitted model was observed to be highly significant as supported by the diagnostics, $F=7.47$ ($P<0.01$), $R^2=0.466$ and the value of Durbin-Watson (D) statistic say 1.92. Thus, the regression model developed for Machi sub-division is given by

Quantity of the rice production = –1881.23–371.47 (area under rice cultivation) + 191.21 (jhum cycle) + 101.10 (size of family + 157.16 (No. of male labour) – 405.18 (No. of female labour) + 27.97 (labour cost) + 63.86 (No. of literate family member).

Table–5.9
Regression coefficients (b) and their significance level undershifting cultivation in Machi sub-division

Explanatory variables	b	S.E	t	P	95%CI for B Lower	Upper
(Constant)**	–1881.23	564.89	–3.33	0.001	–3011.12	–751.34
Area under rice cultivation (in acre)*	–371.47	146.32	–2.54	0.014	–664.16	–78.79
Jhum cycle (in yr)**	191.21	39.05	4.90	0.000	113.09	269.32
Size of family	101.10	89.83	1.13	0.265	–78.58	280.78
No. of male labour	157.16	205.47	0.77	0.447	–253.85	568.17
No. of female labour*	–405.18	171.96	–2.36	0.022	–749.14	–61.21
Labour cost (in '00Rs.)**	27.97	9.35	2.99	0.004	9.27	46.67
No. of literate family member	63.86	86.50	0.74	0.463	–109.17	236.88

* significant at 0.05 probability level;
** significant at 0.01 probability level

The model developed for Tengnoupal sub-division is given by

Quantity of the rice production = –468.47–284.08 (area of agriculture land) + 155.04 (jhum cycle) + 67.35 (size of family) – 133.06 (No. of male labour) + 88.17 (No. of female labour) + 1.14 (labour cost) – 100.93 (No. of literate family member).

Table–5.10
Regression coefficients (b) and their significance level under shifting cultivation in Tengnoupal sub-division

Explanatory variables	b	S.E	t	P	95%CI for B Lower	Upper
(Constant)	–468.47	524.02	–0.89	0.376	–152.21	584.59
Area under rice cultivation (in acre)	–284.08	146.46	–1.94	0.058	–578.40	10.24
Jhum cycle (in yr)**	155.04	36.47	4.25	0.000	81.76	228.32
Size of family	67.35	59.77	1.13	0.265	–52.76	187.47

No. of male labour	–133.06	108.11	–1.23	0.224	–350.31	84.19
No. of female labour	88.17	119.45	0.74	0.464	–151.87	328.21
Labour cost (in '00Rs.)	1.14	5.00	0.23	0.821	–8.92	11.19
No. of literate family member*	–100.93	51.19	–1.99	0.045	–203.79	1.94

* significant at 0.05 probability level;

** significant at 0.01 probability level

In the regression model developed for Tengnoupal sub-division, the constant rice production was –468.47 kg per acre of rice cultivation when the effect of seven independent variables was kept constant (Table–5.10). Two independent variables were significant. As Machi sub-division, jhum cycle was found to be highly significant in the rice production in the Tengnoupal sub-division. It was quantified by regression coefficient, (b =155.04 and S.E=36.47) with 95% CI of 81.76–228.32 and t-value, 4.25 ($P<0.01$). The second significant predictor of the agriculture production in the sub-division was the number of literate family member as quantified by (b=–100.93 and S.E=51.19) with 95% CI of –203.79 to 1.94 and absolute t-value, 1.99 ($P<0.05$). Here, it is interpreted that the rice production is increased by 155 kg corresponding to the each additional one year in jhum cycle when adjusted the effects of other six variables of interest. However, the rice production will be reduced 101 kg to each increase of literate family member in the sub-division. It is obtained when the joint effect of other six independent variables are keeping constant. The regression model for Tengnoupal sub-division was also observed to be significant as evidenced by the diagnostics, F=4.09 ($P<0.01$), R^2=0.37 and D=2.09 (Table–5.10). The fitted model also highlighted that the seven independent variables of interest explained 37of the total variation in the rice production in the Tengnoupal sub-division of Chandel district under shifting cultivation system. Three predictors out of the seven independent variables are observed to have significant impacts on the quantity of the rice production under shifting-cultivation system in Chandel sub-division (Table–5.11).

Table–5.11
Regression coefficients (b) and their significance level under shifting cultivation in Chandel sub-division

Explanatory variables	b	S.E	t	P	95%CI for B Lower	Upper
(Constant)	–184.63	562.80	–0.33	0.744	–131.01	940.39
Area under rice cultivation (in acre)**	–349.05	114.23	–3.06	0.003	-577.39	-120.71
Jhum cycle (in yr)**	109.96	36.84	2.99	0.004	36.33	183.60
Size of family	9.74	59.43	0.16	0.870	–109.05	128.52
No. of male labour	40.19	125.11	0.32	0.749	–209.89	290.27
No. of female labour	79.38	117.44	0.68	0.502	–155.38	314.13
Labour cost(in '00Rs.)*	25.07	11.64	2.15	0.035	1.81	48.34
No. of literate family member	–19.63	54.24	–0.36	0.719	–128.05	88.78

* significant at 0.05 probability level;
** significant at 0.01 probability level

When adjusted the joint effects of the six other independent variables, the rice production significantly decreased by 349.05±114.23 kg per acre (95% CI: –577.39 to –120.71) to each increment of one acre in the area of rice cultivation. It was witnessed by absolute test value (t=3.06, P<0.01). The value of the test statistic, 2.99 (P<0.01) suggested that the rice production was observed to be significantly increased by 109.96 kg per acre (with 95%CI: 36.33–183.60) to each increase of one year in the jhum cycle while adjusted the effects of other six variables – area of agricultural land, family size, number of male labour, number of female labour, labour cost and number of literate family member. Out of the seven predictors of interest, labour cost was also found significant of influenced on the rice production owing to the fact that the rice production would increase by at least 25 kg per acre with 95% CI of 1.81–48.34 corresponding to each increment of rupees one hundred of labour cost. The fitted model was again found to be highly significant as shown by its diagnostics, F=3.08 (P<0.01), D=1.83 and R^2=0.258.

Table–5.12

Regression coefficients (b) and their significance level under shifting cultivation in Chakpikarong sub-division

Explanatory variables	b	S.E	t	P	95%CI for B Lower	Upper
(Constant)	447.21	419.60	1.07	0.289	–384.79	1279.03
Area under rice cultivation (in acre)**	–375.88	107.55	–3.50	0.001	–589.13	–162.64
Jhum cycle (in yr)**	110.61	25.09	4.41	0.000	60.85	160.36
Size of family	–34.84	43.72	–0.80	0.427	–121.52	51.84
No. of male labour	–14.10	94.16	–0.15	0.881	–200.81	172.61
No. of female labour	43.99	84.68	0.52	0.605	–123.91	211.88
Labour cost (in '00Rs.)	2.27	3.01	0.75	0.453	–3.69	8.23
No. of literate family member	43.57	41.44	1.05	0.296	–38.60	125.73

* significant at 0.05 probability level;

** significant at 0.01 probability level

The model also emphasized that the seven variables could explain 26% of the total variation in the rice production of the Chandel sub-division in the present analysis. The fitted model may be expressed as

Quantity of the rice production = –184.63–349.05 (area under rice cultivation) + 109.96 (jhum cycle) + 9.74 (size of family) + 40.19 (No. of male labour) + 79.38 (No. of female labour) + 25.07 (labour cost) – 19.63 (No. of literate family member).

The fitted model for the Chakpikarong sub-division may be given by

Quantity of the rice production = 447.21 – 375.88 (area under rice cultivation) + 110.61 (jhum cycle) – 34.84 (size of family) – 14.10 (No. of male labour) + 43.99 (No. of female labour) + 2.27 (labour cost) + 43.57 (No. of literate family member).

As in the other three sub-divisions (Machi, Tengnoupal,

Chandel) a regression model was also fitted for Chakpikarong sub-division which was highly significant as witnessed by F=4.45 ($P<0.01$), $R^2=0.229$ and D=1.89. In this model the seven independent variables explained 23% of the total variation in the rice production in the sub-division. Only two predictors – area of agriculture land (in acre; $P<0.01$) and jhum cycle (in year; $P<0.01$) had significant effects on the rice production while adjusted the joint effects of other independent variables at their average level (Table–5.12). In this model the constant rice production was 447.21 ± 419.6 kg per acre (with 95% CI: –384.79 to 1279.03) while keeping constant the effects of seven independent variables. The rice production may be increased by 110.61 ± 25.09 kg per acre of land (with 95% CI: 60.85–160.36) to each increment of one year in jhum cycle when adjusted the effects of six other variables – area of agricultural land, family size, number of male labour, number of female labour, labour cost and number of literate family member. In similar patterns of other sub-divisions, the rice production might significantly be reduced by 375.88 kg to each increase of one acre of area under rice cultivation as supported by test (t) value, 3.5 ($P<0.01$) (Table–5.12).

5.6.3 Stepwise Models under Shifting-Cultivation

The step-wise method of regression analysis was again applied to identify most influential variables on the variation in the rice production in 4 sub-divisions namely, Machi, Tengnoupal, Chandel and Chakpikarong in isolation. Here, seven independent variables were included in the analysis. They are area under rice cultivation (in acre), Jhum cycle (in year), number of male labour engaged in rice cultivation, number of female labour engaged in rice cultivation, labour cost (in '00 Rs.), number of literate persons in the family and size of family.

In Machi sub-division the last model can be achieved in fourth step. The most influential explanatory variables in the sub-population were jhum cycle ($P<0.01$), labour cost ($P<0.01$), area of cultivated land ($P<0.05$) (Table–5.13A) and number of literate family member ($P<0.05$). In the last fitted model, the constant rice production was –1795.13 568.88 kg per acre (with 95% CI: –2931.95 to –658.31) while keeping constant the effects of four explanatory variables. Further, the model interprets that the rice production is increased by 180.90 kg per acre (95% CI: 104.98–256.82) with standard error of 37.99 kg to each increase of one year in jhum cycle while adjusted the joint effect of three variables – labour cost, area of cultivated land and number of literate family member. It was highly significant as supported by the test (t) value of 4.76 ($P<0.01$).

In this last model to each increment of rupees one hundred in labour cost, the rice production increased by 26.73 kg per acre (95%CI: 8.33–45.13) when adjusted the joint effect of three variables namely jhum cycle, area of agriculture land and number of literate family member. Keeping constant the effects of three variables – jhum cycle, labour cost and number of literate family member, increase in the area under cultivation reduced rice production may be reduced by 364.75 kg per acre (with 95%CI: –658.69 to –70.81) which was significant ($t=2.48$, $P<0.05$). In the similar way, the rice production increased by 141.99 64.93 kg per acre (with 95% CI: 12.25–271.74) with the every addition of on literate family member, after controlled the three other predictors. The fitted model of Machi sub-division was highly significant ($F=10.60$, $P<0.01$ and $D=1.86$) (Table–5.14). The significant four variables explained 40% of the total variation in the rice production in the sub-division, as witnessed by the R^2 value (=0.402) which was gradually increased from 0.223 ($F=18.91$, $P<0.01$).

In Tengnoupal sub-division only two predictors say, jhum cycle and area of cultivated land were observed to be significant, as witnessed by the regression coefficient, 151.40 with 95% CI: 84.92–217.88 ($t=4.57$, $P<0.01$) and –286.81 with 95% CI: –564.53 to –9.08 ($t=2.07$, $P<0.05$) respectively (Table–5.13A). Here, the two predictors explained 28% of the total variation in the rice production ($R^2 = 0.279$) manifested in Table–5.13A and Table–5.13B.

Table–5.13(A)

Stepwise regression coefficients (b) and their significance level under shifting-cultivation in Machi and Tengnoupal sub-divisions

Sub-Division	Model	Explanatory variables	b	S.E	t	P	95%CI for B Lower	95%CI for B Upper
Machi	1	(Constant)	-887.02	523.97	-1.69	0.095	-1933.17	159.13
		Jhum cycle**	160.68	36.95	4.35	0.000	86.91	234.46
	2	(Constant)*	-1175.93	506.67	-2.32	0.023	-2187.83	-164.04
		Jhum cycle**	139.91	35.76	3.91	0.000	68.49	211.32
		Labour cost**	26.70	9.20	2.90	0.005	8.32	45.08
	3	(Constant)*	-1127.88	494.13	-2.28	0.026	-2115.02	-140.74
		Jhum cycle **	177.34	39.06	4.54	0.000	99.30	255.38
		Labour cost*	22.11	9.22	2.40	0.019	3.69	40.54
		Area of agriculture land*	-317.06	149.70	-2.12	0.038	-616.13	-17.99
	4	(Constant)**	-1795.13	568.88	-3.16	0.002	-2931.95	-658.31
		Jhum cycle**	180.90	37.99	4.76	0.000	104.98	256.82
		Labour cost**	26.73	9.21	2.90	0.005	8.33	45.13
		Area of agriculture land*	-364.75	147.09	-2.48	0.016	-658.69	-70.81
		No. of literate family member*	141.99	64.93	2.19	0.032	12.25	271.74

Sub-Division	Model	Explanatory variables	b	S.E	t	P	95%CI for B Lower	Upper
Tengnoupal	1	(Constant)*	-324.17	421.91	-0.77	0.446	-1169.69	521.34
		Jhum cycle**	116.75	29.47	3.96	0.000	57.69	175.80
	2	(Constant)	-338.29	409.89	-0.83	0.413	-1160.07	483.50
		Jhum cycle**	151.40	33.16	4.57	0.000	84.92	217.88
		Area of agriculture land*	-286.81	138.53	-2.07	0.043	-564.53	-9.08

Table–5.13 (B)

Stepwise regression coefficients (b) and their significance level under shifting-cultivation in Chandel and Chakpikarong sub-divisions

Sub-Division	Model	Explanatory variables	b	S.E	t	P	95%CI for B Lower	Upper
Chandel	1	(Constant)**	1788.55	205.07	8.72	0.000	1379.33	2197.76
		Area under rice cultivation*	-227.00	108.80	-2.09	0.041	-444.10	-9.91
	2	(Constant)	434.83	468.94	0.93	0.357	-501.19	1370.84
		Jhum cycle**	113.60	35.88	3.17	0.002	41.99	185.21
		Area under rice cultivation**	-360.94	110.63	-3.26	0.002	-581.76	-140.13
	3	(Constant)	-0.67	491.33	-0.00	0.999	-981.64	980.30
		Jhum cycle**	116.03	34.77	3.34	0.001	46.62	185.45
		Labour cost*	24.61	10.58	2.33	0.023	3.48	45.74
		Area under rice cultivation**	-379.12	107.45	-3.53	0.001	-593.64	-164.60

Sub-Division	Model	Explanatory variables	b	S.E	t	P	95%CI for B Lower	95%CI for B Upper
Chakpik-arong	1	(Constant)	224.31	347.74	0.65	0.520	-464.75	913.37
		Jhum cycle**	86.30	24.40	3.54	0.001	37.94	134.65
	2	(Constant)	435.80	333.38	1.31	0.194	-224.89	1096.48
		Jhum cycle**	114.39	24.23	4.72	0.000	66.37	162.42
		Area under rice cultivation**	-392.38	103.88	-3.78	0.000	-598.24	-186.52

* significant at 0.05 probability level;

** significant at 0.01 probability level

In Chandel sub-division the best model could be achieved in third step with three explanatory variables – jhum cycle (P<0.01), labour cost (P<0.05) and area under rice cultivation (P<0.01) (Table–5.13 B). In this fitted third model, the best model for Chandel sub-division was equal to – 0.67 + 116.03 (jhum cycle) + 24.61 (labour cost) – 379.12 (area under rice cultivation).

The fitted model highlighted that the rice production was increased by 116.03 ± 34.77 kg per acre (95 %CI: 46.62–185.45) to each increment of one year in jhum cycle which was highly significant, evidenced by the t-value, 3.34 (P<0.01), while adjusting the joint effect two independent variables namely, labour cost and area of agriculture land. The rice production under analysis increased by 24.61kg (95% CI: 3.48–45.74) per acre corresponding to each increment of rupees one hundred of labour cost while adjusted the effect of jhum cycle and area of agriculture land in the sub-division. The best model of Chandel sub-division was also found to be highly significant (F=7.12, P<0.01 and D=1.67) and the three variables explained at least 24% of the total variation in the rice production in the sub-division, as witnessed by the R^2 value (=0.244) which was gradually increased in the three steps from 0.060 (F=4.35, P<0.05) (Table–5.14).

Table–5.14
Model Summary of Stepwise regression analysis according to Sub-Division under shifting cultivation

Sub-division	Model	R^2	Adjusted R^2	Durbin Watson (D)	F-value	P-value
Machi	1	0.223	0.211	1.86	18.91	<0.01
	2	0.312	0.291		14.73	<0.01
	3	0.357	0.327		11.84	<0.01
	4	0.402	0.364		10.60	<0.01
Tengnoupal	1	0.222	0.208	2.03	15.70	<0.01
	2	0.279	0.253		10.46	<0.01
Chandel	1	0.060	0.046	1.67	4.35	<0.05
	2	0.183	0.158		7.48	<0.01

	3	0.244	0.210		7.12	<0.01
Chakpikarong	1	0.101	0.093	1.87	12.51	<0.01
	2	0.204	0.190		14.14	<0.01

As in the three other sub-divisions, the best model of Chakpikarong sub-division was highly significant (Model test, F=14.14, P<0.01 and D=1.87) with two explanatory variables – jhum cycle and area under rice cultivation which could explain 20% of the total variation in the rice production as evidenced by the R^2 value (=0.204) which was increased from 0.101 (F=12.51, P<0.01) shown in Table–5.14. The fitted model of the Chakpikarong sub-division may be expressed by the rice production which equal to 435.80 + 114.39 (jhum cycle) – 392.38 (area of agriculture land). The fitted model revealed that the rice production was increased by 114.39 kg per acre (95% CI: 66.37–162.42) with standard error of 24.23 kg corresponding to one year increase in jhum cycle when controlled the effect of the area under rice cultivation which was found to be highly significant, evidenced by the t-value say 4.72 (P<0.01) noted in Table–5.13(B). However, the rice production reduced by 392.38 kg (95% CI: –598.24 to –186.52) per acre to each increment of one acre of area under rice cultivation in the Chakpikarong sub-division. It was also highly significant (t=3.78; P<0.01).

To conclude, out of eleven explanatory variables specified only two variables – area under rice cultivation and irrigation facility were significant in the wet-cultivation system in Chandel district. The impact of area under rice cultivation was negative. It implies that in the hilly slope it is increasingly difficult to cultivate with the additional size of area under cultivation and hence the production of rice declines instead of increase. It may also be due to negligence of farmers with larger size of holdings. When regressions were run for four sub-divisions it was found that area under rice cultivation, irrigation facility and cost of fertilizers were significant in Machi; only irrigation facility was significant in Tengnoupal sub-division; irrigation facility and labour cost were significant in Chandel sub-division and number of female labour and irrigation facility were significant in Chakpikarong sub-division. The positive sign of labour cost in Chandel sub-division and fertilizer in Machi sub-division indicate that the higher production of rice might be resulted from substitution of these higher cost factors by other factors which have lower prices. The above analysis reveals that striking significance of irrigation facility for the increase of rice production in the district as well as in all sub-divisions of the district.

In the regression analysis of rice production under shifting cultivation, out of seven independent variables only three variables (area under rice cultivation, jhum cycle and labour cost) were significant in Chandel district. When regression analysis was made for different sub-divisions of the district, four explanatory variables (area under rice cultivation, jhum cycle, number of female labour and labour cost) were found significant in Machi sub-division. Two variables (jhum cycle and number of literate family members) in Tengnoupal sub-divisions, three variables (area under rice cultivation, jhum cycle and labour cost) in Chandel sub-division, two variables (area under rice cultivationand jhum cycle) in ChakpiKarong sub-division were found significant.

6

Chapter

Fertility Dynamics and Socio-Demographic Variables

6.1 Introduction

There has been a general agreement among economists and demographers that higher level of economic development or higher income leads to lower fertility. But there has been limited study on the impact of fertility on economic development. In spite of it, it is very clear that the decline in fertility brings improvement in economic conditions at both macro and micro levels. At macro level the reduction in fertility would mean lower number of children in the economy. As a result of this the same amount of government expenditure would create higher level of per capita expenditure on different levels of government budget and create more welfare and development of the economy. Similarly, at micro level too standard of living of the household will improve because of the same reason of decline in fertility. In this context, it is very much pertinent to examine what are the socio-economic factors which determine fertility rate for the economic development of Chandel district in Manipur.

The actual reproductive performance of a woman or a group of women is generally termed as human fertility. Its measurement in a community is provided by the actual number of live births to a group of women during a given period of time. Human fertility is influenced by a large number of socio-economic, demographic and cultural factors, such as caste, type of family, religion, place of residence, income, educational level, employment status, occupation, sex preference, age at menarche, age at marriage, lactation, fetal death, infant and child mortality, age at delivery etc. (Patnaik, 1985; Singh, 2002; Nath et. al., 2004; Singh et. al., 2012). Moreover, fertility is highly susceptible to human control by both deliberate action and effects of behaviour not consciously be directed to this purpose. In many communities, couples are typically conditioned to desire a given number of boy(s) and girl(s) depending on a number of factors. In fact, human fertility is basically a complex physiological process but child bearing in any society is influenced by many socio-economic, demographic and cultural setups of the society.

A good number of past findings have observed that human fertility may vary from place to place, society to society, community to community and within a society or community itself. In industrialized countries the fertility rate is low while in agricultural and developing countries it is comparatively high. The pattern of fertility variation in different countries is heterogeneous because of their paramount constituents of socio-economic, demographic, ecological and cultural factors. According to Patnaik (1985), fertility rates are very low in Europeans other developed countries where individualism dominates the mode of living, people are highly educated, economic condition is sound, standard of living is high and people are exposed well to mass media. On the other hand, there is always prevalence of high fertility in developing countries like India where society is primarily agricultural, traditional and joint family oriented has high percentage of people living below poverty line and low educational status (Bhagat and Chattopadhyay, 2004; Nanda, 2005; Saha, 2006; Kumar et al, 2012; Singh et al., 2013).

The fertility indices in India have been affected by the different sections of community. The pattern of fertility dynamics is problematic among the tribal communities too. According to NFHS-3, the fertility rate of scheduled tribes was higher (3.1 children per women) than that of national level (2.7) in 2005-06. The report also highlighted that the fertility rates was observed 2.9 for scheduled caste and 2.8 for other backward classes. Population scientists have illustrated many possible causes of higher tribal fertility. Guntupalli (2007) has revealed that tribal populations are far behind from the mainstream of society in many socio-economic characteristics. The findings of Abhimanyu (2012) reveal that tribal people have lower level of education, status of women and exposure to mass media. They also have lower age at marriage and lower family planning acceptance, and higher fertility and mortality rates. A large majority of women particularly tribal women get married before reaching the minimum legal age at marriage. The use of family planning methods is low among tribal women, although almost all women know at least one method of contraception. And hence, it leads high fertility (Kumar et al., 2012). Chandel district of Manipur is not an exception to the variation of fertility in complex form. Thus, the investigation of fertility variation in the district under study with respect to socio-economic and demographic characters is very interesting area which has important implication for future economic development in the district. Here, the considered socio-demographic factors are place of residence, type of family, educational level, employment status, income, sex preference, age at marriage, age at delivery etc.

6.2 Fertility and Place of Residence

The place of residence in developing societies usually determines people's life styles and perceptions of the global context, economic, social, cultural and political activities. It is one of the socio-economic factors affecting fertility level (Mahadevan, 1979; Patnaik, 1985; Singh, 2002; Singh et al., 2012). The study of fertility is influenced by place of residence in India has assumed a special significance in recent years in view of the problem emanating from rapid population growth. The concept of urban residence as it is understood in the West is different in context of Manipur society. Even if the couples have urban residence, they often continue to have link with rural areas by way of economic interest there. In the present context, urban-rural differential is defined according to Population of Manipur' 2006 (Directorate of Economics and Statistic, Govt. of Manipur, 2008).

Table–6.1
Fertility differential according to place of residence

Place of residence	No. of households (in %)	Mean ± S.D	95%CI for mean	Test values
Rural	87.9	3.27 ± 1.84	3.08–3.47	t=0.76,
Urban	12.1	3.49 ± 2.03	2.91–4.07	P>0.05
Total	**100**	**3.30 ± 1.86**	**3.12–3.48**	

In the present analysis, it is observed from Table–6.1 that the number of eligible mothers in urban and rural areas were 12.1% and 87.9% respectively. Without considering the effects of other factors, the mean fertility in urban area was found to be 3.49 ± 2.03 with 95% CI: 2.91–4.07 and that of rural area, 3.27 ± 1.84 with 95% CI: 3.08–3.47. The mean fertility of the total population, 3.30 ± 1.86 was found to be insignificantly different with place of residence, as evidenced by t-value (0.76, P>0.05) at 5% probability level of significance. The statistical insignificance is due to lack of urban characteristics in the urban areas in the district.

The study population is categorized into four sub-divisions namely Tengnoupal (33.6%), Machi (34.5%), Chandel (12.2%) and Chakpikarong (19.7%) manifested in Table–6.2. While the overall average fertility was 3.30 ± 1.86 with 95% CI: 3.12–3.48, the highest mean fertility of 3.77 ± 1.99 with 95% CI: 3.33–4.22 was observed in Chakpikarong and the lowest level of 3.10 ± 1.46 (95% CI: 2.68–3.53) was observed in Chandel district. This distribution of the average fertility was statistical insignificant. It was evidenced by F-value, 2.16 (P>0.05). The statistical insignificance is explained by the fact that socio-economic characteristics of these sub-divisions are almost the same.

Table–6.2
Fertility differential according to Sub-Division

Sub-Division	No. of house-holds (in %)	Mean ± S.D	95%CI for mean	Test values
Tengnoupal	33.6	3.21 ± 2.03	2.86–3.55	F=2.16,
Machi	34.5	3.19 ± 1.71	2.90–3.48	P>0.05
Chandel	12.2)	3.10 ± 1.46	2.68–3.53	
Chakpika-rong	19.7	3.77 ± 1.99	3.33–4.22	
Total	**100**	**3.30 ± 1.86**	**3.12–3.48**	

6.3 Fertility and Type of Family

The institution of joint family as well as nuclear family is considered to be one of the important factors influencing on the rate of fertility in India. In the present analysis, nuclear family refers to the family consisting of husband, wife and their own children only. All types of families other than nuclear one may be considered as joint or extended family. Survey data revealed that 96.8% of the eligible couples belong to nuclear family and the rest, 3.2% to joint family (Table–6.3). The mean fertility measured in terms of average number of children ever born to joint family was found to be 2.83 ± 1.53 with 95% CI: 1.86–3.80 which was lower than that of nuclear family, 3.32 ± 1.87 with 95%CI: 3.13–3.50. The variation in the mean fertility according to type of family was not significant (t=0.88, P>0.05). It may be concluded that there is no difference in the mean fertility of joint family and that of nuclear ones in the population irrespective of the effects of other factors under study. Generally, the couples adopted nuclear family after spending a considerable duration of time with their parents as joint family. In addition to this, they establish nuclear family after having some children.

Table–6.3
Fertility differential according to type of family

Type of Family	No. of house-holds (in %)	Mean ± S.D	95%CI for mean	Test values
Nuclear	96.8	3.32 ± 1.87	3.13–3.50	t= 0.88,
Joint	3.2	2.83 ± 1.53	1.86–3.80	P>0.05
Total	**100**	**3.30 ± 1.86**	**3.12–3.48**	

6.4 Fertility and Different Community and Religion

The caste system is historically pivotal factor in the stratification of Indian society which share in slow growth of social development in the country. It is generally considered as a social stratification variable in the studies of differential reproductive performance for various reasons. Patnaik (1985) observes the average birth performance of the upper caste is lower than that of the backward caste or scheduled caste. As mentioned elsewhere, social stratification by caste system in Manipur is not strict as in other parts of the country. The Meities – original inhabitants of Manipur, the Brahmins, the scheduled caste, and scheduled tribe live together in various parts of the State. Moreover, in contrast to the caste prejudices in some other parts of India, the scheduled caste and scheduled tribe are not untouchable sections of the population in the community. Also, there is no practically untouchable community in the state of Manipur in general and Chandel district in particular.

Table–6.4
Fertility differential according to name of tribes/community

Name of tribes/ community	No. of house-holds (in %)	Mean ± S.D	95%CI for mean	Test values
Kuki	28.5	3.77 ± 2.18	3.37–4.18	F=2.90,
Chothe	11.9	2.06 ± 1.01	1.53–2.59	P<0.05
Maring	15.8	3.12 ± 1.75	2.85–3.38	
Lamkang	7.1	4.00 ± 1.71	3.09–4.91	

Tarao	4.9	3.00 ± 1.21	2.23–3.77
Moyon	5.2	2.83 ± 1.34	1.98–3.68
Monsang	6.6	2.53 ± 1.55	1.67–3.39
Anal	12.1	3.52 ± 1.83	2.80–4.24
Non-Local/ Tribal	7.9	3.40 ± 1.40	2.62–4.18
Total	**100**	**3.30 ± 1.86**	**3.12–3.48**

The variation in the average fertility has been investigated according to different tribes/communities residing in the population under study in this section. Here, nine different communities were included. They were Kuki, Chothe, Maring, Lamkang, Tarao, Moyon, Monsang, Anal, and Non-Local/Tribal. The findings highlighted the fertility level in Lamkang tribe (7.1%) was the highest, with 95% CI: 3.09–4.91 followed by Kuki (28.5 percent) with 3.77 ± 2.18 (95% CI: 3.37–4.18) and the lowest fertility of 2.06 ± 1.01 with 95% CI: 1.53–2.59 was observed in Chothe tribe (11.9%) shown in Table–6.4.

The mean fertility of below three live birth were observed in three tribes namely Chothe (2.06 ± 1.01 with 95% CI: 1.53–2.59), Moyon (2.83 ± 1.34 with 95% CI: 1.98–3.68), and Monsang (2.53 ± 1.55 with 95% CI: 1.67–3.39). The remaining six tribes/communities viz., Kuki (3.77 ± 2.18), Maring (3.12 ± 1.75), Lamkang (4 ± 1.71), Tarao (3 ± 1.21), Anal (3.52 ± 1.83), and Non-Local/Tribal (3.40 ± 1.40) had their fertility level of more than three live births while the overall average fertility was 3.3 ± 1.86 with 95% CI: 3.12–3.48. Irrespective of the joint effects of other factors under investigation, the variation in the average fertility was found to be statistically significant as witnessed by F-value, 2.90 ($P<0.05$). The lower fertility levels observed in three communities may perhaps be linked with a number of other socio-demographic factors like educational level, infrastructure available, employment etc.

Table–6.4a
Fertility differential according to religion

Religion	No. of house-holds (in %)	Mean ± S.D	95%CI for mean	Test values
Christian	96.6	3.30 ± 1.87	3.12–3.49	t=0.14,
Non-Christian	3.4	3.23 ± 1.59	2.27–4.19	P>0.05
Total	**100**	**3.30 ± 1.86**	**3.12–3.48**	

Categorizing the eligible mothers under investigation by their religion category – Christian and Non-Christian, the fertility of 3.23 ± 1.59 with 95% CI of 2.27–4.19 live births of non-Christian was visibly lower than that of Christian mothers, 3.30 ± 1.87 with 95% CI of 3.12–3.40 live births (Table–6.4a). The variation in the mean fertility was confirmed to be statistically insignificant as quantified by its lower test (t) value, 0.14 at 5% probability level of significance. The insignificance of t-value might be explained by two factors. These two religion groups reside in the same socio-economic environment and they get the same health facilities available in the district.

6.5 Fertility and Educational Level

A good number of past findings witnessed that the educational level of couples has a significant linkage with the variation in fertility level in many communities (Mahadevan, 1979; Patnaik, 1985; Srinivasan, 2002; Singh et al., 2007; Singh et al., 2012). An inverse relationship between fertility and educational level appeared both in United States and countries in Europe in the late nineteenth century. This relationship is now diminishing or even disappearing in some low fertility countries. In developing countries like India, mother's education has been considered to have a strong effect on mortality of young children (Rao et al., 1997; Das and Dey, 2003). The educated mothers have ensured healthier environment, nutritious food and knowledge of better health care facilities for children than non-literate mothers. In India, education may be a direct and powerful indicator of the women's status. Through these variables mother's education has negative impact on fertility. Moreover, the relationship between education and fertility is complex one. It is intricately associated with many socio-economic factors and attitudes. In many studies, it is found that education depresses fertility by rising marriage age, strengthen the propensity to be worker, fosters a favourable attitude towards small family norm and improves awareness and encourages the use of family planning methods. Some studies have also depicted clearly the impact of female education on reduction of fertility (Akmam, 2002; Singh et al, 2012). In this section, the variation in the mean fertility is analysed according to the educational level of couples under investigation. For the present study, the couple's educational achievement is categorized into five levels – illiterate, literate but under matriculate, matriculate but below 10+2, 10+2 but under graduate, and graduate and above. In the present analysis, the inverse relationship was found between educational level of spouses and the mean fertility (Table–6.5 and 6.5a).

Table–6.5
Fertility differential according to educational level of male spouse

Educational Level	No. of house-holds (in %)	Mean ± S.D	95%CI for mean	Test values
Illiterate	14.8	3.76 ± 1.79	3.20–4.32	F=1.04,
Literate but under matriculate	49.8	3.30 ± 1.81	3.00–3.60	P>0.05
Matriculate but below 10+2	17.9	3.32 ± 1.91	2.78–3.86	
10+2 but under graduate	5.8	3.24 ± 2.02	2.20–4.27	
Graduate and above	11.7	2.91 ± 1.71	2.29–3.52	
Total	**100**	**3.30 ± 1.86**	**3.12–3.48**	

The highest mean fertility of 3.76 ± 1.79 with 95% CI: 3.20–4.32 was found in the illiterate husband and the lowest fertility, 2.91 ± 1.71 (95% CI: 2.29–3.52) was noted in the husbands who had the education qualifications of graduate and above while the overall mean fertility in the district was 3.30 ± 1.86 (95% CI: 3.12–3.48). The similar pattern of variation in the fertility was also found according to the level of education achieved by the wife. The highest mean fertility, 3.47 ± 2.03 (95% CI: 3.04–3.90) was observed in the illiterate wife and lowest fertility of 2.87 ± 1.73 (95% CI: 1.91–3.82) was however found in the women who had at least graduate. It shows that the fertility level gradually declines with the improvement in the level of couple's education, despite insignificant variation in the average fertility. The insignificant variation might perhaps be caused by the joint effects of other factors under analysis in the sense that education may work on the variation in the fertility as an intermediate factors. In other words, though couples with higher educational qualification had higher knowledge of modern health facility, favourable attitude towards small family norms, modern family planning methods etc. they might not be able to overcome the hindrance given by transport and communication, religion, cultural values, actually available medical facility and economic conditions.

Table–6.5a
Fertility differential according to educational level of female spouse

Educational Level	No. of house-holds (in %)	Mean ± S.D	95%CI for mean	Test values
Illiterate	20.8	3.47 ± 2.03	3.04–3.90	F=0.78,
Literate but under matriculate	46.4	3.26 ± 1.59	2.74–3.77	P>0.05
Matriculate but below 10+2	19.8	3.00 ± 1.23	2.59-3.41	
10+2 but under graduate	8.3	2.89 ± 1.69	1.59–4.19	

Graduate and above	4.7	2.87 ± 1.73	1.91–3.82
Total	**100**	**3.30 ± 1.86**	**3.12–3.48**

6.6 Fertility and Employment Status

Employment of women outside the home is found to be negatively associated to their fertility level (Singh, 2002; Singh, 2009; Singh et al, 2012). Once the woman became economically independent by way of employment, it is just believed that the fertility of those employed women may result in lower fertility than that of unemployed or non-working women. The reason of low fertility among employed women may be attributed to their better education, good economic conditions, better standard of living and also late marriage. The employment status was categorised into two categories viz., no government employee in the family (unemployed) and at least one government employee in the family (employed). Here, the term government employee referred only to those persons who worked either in government or in semi-government or in even organised sector having a good regular income. All the persons other than the employed ones were treated as unemployed.

Table–6.6
Fertility differential according to employment status of family members

Employment Status	No. of house-holds (in %)	Mean ± S.D	95%CI for mean	Test values
No Govt. employee in the family	92.7	3.36 ± 1.89	3.16–3.55	t=2.16,
At least one Govt. employee in the family	7.3	2.59 ± 1.32	2.08–3.09	P<0.05
Total	**100**	**3.30 ± 1.86**	**3.12–3.48**	

It is observed that the mean fertility of the employed group (7.3%) was found to be 2.59 ± 1.32 with 95% CI: 2.08–3.09

against that of unemployed group (92.7%), 3.36 ± 1.89 with 95% CI: 3.16–3.55, while the overall average fertility was 3.3 ± 1.86. This variation in the average fertility was confirmed to be significantly varied with employment status of the couples under investigation. It was evidenced by the value of t (2.16, $P<0.05$). Thus, it is confirmed that employment status of family members is an important factor in determining the level of fertility in Chandel district.

6.7 Fertility and Income Level

Many studies have found that the fertility decreases as income increases in India. Reddy (1984) finds that income is directly related to attitudes to family planning irrespective of caste. However, Singh (1989) does not reveal any regular gradations in various indices of fertility with respect to various income groups. On the other hand, Patnaik (1985) observes no inverse relationship between fertility and income in the sense that as income goes up from the lowest conceivable limit, fertility also tends to rise progressively up to a certain level, indicating a marked variation of positive correlation between the two. However, beyond that level of income, there appears to be a tendency for fertility to decline. This tends to suggest that minimum level economic prosperity may be essential for the decline in fertility. Similar findings can be seen in the studies of Nahar and Rahman (2006), Singh et al. (2010), and Singh et al. (2012), Harvinder (2000). In the present context, the variation in the fertility level has been investigated in relation to different income level of the population under study. For analysis purpose, the family income in the district was categorized into six classes, say below Rs. 5,000; Rs. 5,000-10,000; Rs. 10,000-15,000; Rs. 15,000-20,000; Rs. 20,000-25,000; and Rs. 25,000 and above depicted in Table–6.7.

Table–6.7

Fertility differential according to monthly income

Monthly Income (in '000Rs.)	No. of households (in %)	Mean ± S.D	95%CI for mean	Test values
<5	47.12	3.34 ± 1.82	3.08–3.60	r=-0.09,
5-10	17.54	3.56 ± 1.85	3.12–4.00	P>0.05
10-15	6.77	3.30 ± 1.44	2.73–3.86	F=1.12,
15-20	8.27	3.52 ± 2.17	2.75–4.28	P>0.05
20-25	5.76	2.87 ± 1.77	2.11–3.63	
25+	14.54	2.91 ± 2.01	2.38–3.44	
Total	**100**	**3.30 ± 1.86**	**3.12–3.48**	

The higher fertility level of above three live birth was observed in the families with lower income levels of below Rs. 20,000 and the lower fertility of below three live birth was witnessed in the family of comparatively higher income group of above Rs. 20,000. The highest fertility level of 3.56 ± 1.85 live births with 95% CI: 3.12–4.00 was observed in the family with level of monthly income, Rs. 5,000–10,000 and the lowest fertility of 2.87 ± 1.77 live births (95% CI: 2.11–3.63) was found in the income class of Rs. 20,000–25,000.

Without considering the effects of other factors under investigation, the variation in the average fertility in the population was found to be insignificantly varied with family income. It was witnessed by F-value, 1.12 (P>0.05). The present finding supports the hypothesis that mean fertility bears an inverse relationship with family income (r=–0.09) but it is not statistically significant (P>0.05). In this bi-variate analysis, the relationship between fertility and income may perhaps not be found due to influences of many other intermediate variables which have also been explained in earlier section. But, from this pattern of variation, it may be inferred that the couple of certain higher income groups who are generally educated and more exposed to different media of communication experience lower fertility.

6.8 Fertility and Age at Marriage

The term marriage is a social institutional binding of a man with a woman to fulfill their sexual urge which has close relation to the process of reproduction. In India, all births occur within the institution of marriage and the proportion of illegitimate births is negligible. Low age at marriage has adverse consequences on population growth, maternal and child health and women's life, especially women's status. It may be noted that even if fertility approaches to replacement level after the year 2010 in some southern states, absolute number of population would continue to increase for many years because of population momentum in India (Singh et al., 2012). Population momentum is an effect of high fertility in the recent past, which thus produced a large population base leading to an enormous number of young women entering into reproductive age. One way of reducing the effect of population momentum is to rise the age at marriage of women.

The past findings have shown that children born to young mothers have a higher chance of mortality and the maternal mortality is also high among young mothers (Choe et al., 2005). Many past evidences highlights that early marriage and subsequent childbearing at an early age hamper biological and mental development of women. Due to early childbearing, biological growth of young women cannot occur in full potential because of maternal drainage during pregnancy and lactation. Moreover, repeated pregnancies beginning in early age adversely affect women's health through maternal depletion syndrome. Early age at marriage negatively affects women's status. Husband and in-laws dominate over young wives on decision making about desired family size, use of contraceptives, and use of reproductive health services (Heaton, 1996, Shawky and Milaat, 2001). Given the culture of early marriage and early childbearing, its negative consequences on population momentum and on maternal and child mortality, family planning and reproductive health programme can reduce maternal and child mortality through appropriate and effective contraceptive methods supplied to young married or newly wed couples. However, recent past studies show that contraceptive use among young married women is low.

In this context, the variation in the fertility level has been analysed according to age at marriage of wife. As a method, the female spouses in the population have been clubbed into six categories of their completed ages at marriage namely, below 18 years, 18-20 years, 21-23 years, 24-26 years, 27-29 years and 30 years and above shown with different fertility levels (Table–6.8). In this analysis too, the variation in the average fertility was negatively related with age at marriage of female spouse ($r = -0.20$, $P<0.01$).

Table–6.8
Fertility differential according to female age at marriage

Age at marriage (in yr)	No. of households (in %)	Mean ± S.D	95%CI for mean	Test values
<18	15.3	4.17 ± 1.81	3.72–4.63	r=–0.201;
18-20	33.3	3.02 ± 1.96	2.69–3.35	P<0.01
21-23	20.2	3.67 ± 1.73	3.30–4.05	F=8.19,
24-26	5.6	3.37 ± 1.62	2.96–3.78	P<0.01
27-29	6.1	2.80 ± 1.56	2.16–3.44	
30+	9.5	1.97 ± 1.52	1.40–2.53	
Total	**100**	**3.30 ± 1.86**	**3.12–3.48**	

The highest mean fertility of 4.17 ± 1.81 with 95% CI: 3.72–4.63 was observed among the women who married at the age below 18 years. It was followed by those who married at 21-23 years of their age. In this distribution of mean fertility according to female's completed age at marriage, the lowest fertility of 1.97 ± 1.52 with 95% CI: 1.40–2.53 was observed in the women who got married at the age group of 30 years and above. Again, the mean fertility was found to vary highly and significantly according to their ages at marriage in the population as evidenced by F-value (8.19) at 0.01 probability level of significance. The pattern of variation is supported by the past findings (Patnaik, 1985; Shawky and Milaat, 2001; Singh et al., 2009; Singh et al., 2013).

6.9 Fertility and Age at First Delivery

A dramatic fertility decline in South-eastern Asia in recent decades partly was due to women postponing marriage and the birth of the first child (Prachuabmoh, 2002). The women age at first delivery in developing countries has also important consequences on the demographic characters of the population (Rajaretnam, 1990) and these variables are important indicators of women's status and for evolving gender roles too. A couple who intend to have one or two children may want to lengthen the space between marriage and first birth in order to better establish their life as a couple, and this would give more time for training and work experience before the first child arrives (Martin, 1995). Thus, the lengthening of the interval between marriage and first birth may be in the interest of individual couples (Zheng, 2000).

India has achieved a little success in the reduction of fertility and child mortality and lower population growth rate in the last two decades. The National Population Policy (NPP)-2000, National Health Policy (NHP)-2002 and further National Rural Health Mission (NRHM)-2005 have much emphasised on bringing down the fertility from the current level to the replacement level (2.1). Even if fertility approaches to replacement level in the near future, absolute number of population will continue to increase for many years because of population momentum. The impact of persistently low age at marriage on maintaining the high fertility rate is now well recognized in India. Though, female age at marriage in India has been rising slowly since around the middle of the last century, the current level is low in comparison to most low fertility countries. There is a significant variation in the age at marriage among the states especially between the northern and southern states, and within states among castes, communities and other social sections. It is well known that direct implementation of the law and legislation may not be feasible in the backward states having low level of female education, rather government can approach through only factors that are amenable to social intervention. In this context it is important to know the recent changes in the female effective age at marriage in various states of India and identify the causal factors that are associated with low level of female age at marriage in the Indian states. In some rural parts of India, the first birth is usually delayed because of temporary separation of married partners with the female partners going over to their parents' place for some time even after marriage. This social custom plays an important role in delaying the first birth (Kumar and Danabalan, 2006). Early child bearing contributes to population growth in two ways. First, in the absence of any intentional contraceptive practices, women who begin bearing children early in their life have more births than equally fecund women who begin so at older ages and secondly, child births occurring at younger ages imply a higher rate of fertility and population growth because of the shorter length of time between generations (Teachman and Heckert, 1985). The present section is devoted to examine the impact of age at delivery on the variation in average fertility in the district under study.

Table–6.9
Fertility differential according to age of women at first delivery

Age at delivery	No. of households (in %)	Mean ± S.D	95%CI for mean	Test values
<18	14.4	4.19 ± 1.80	3.72–4.67	r=–0.246,
18-20	14.0	3.70 ± 1.83	3.22–4.19	P<0.01
21-23	42.1	3.12 ± 1.93	2.82–3.42	F=6.29,
24-26	15.6	3.27 ± 1.55	2.88–3.66	P<0.01
27-29	5.6	3.09 ± 1.86	2.28–3.89	
30+	8.3	2.18 ± 1.49	1.65–2.71	
Total	**100**	**3.30 ± 1.86**	**3.12–3.48**	

The fertility varied inversely with the age at first delivery

($r=-0.25, P<0.01$) irrespective of the effects of other variables under consideration. This shows that there was significantly and negatively linear relationship between fertility and the age at their first delivery. Fertility gradually declined from 4.19 ± 1.8 with 95%CI: 3.72–4.67 of women who delivered their first child at below 18 years of their age to 2.18 ± 1.49 (95% CI: 1.65–2.71) of the women issuing first delivery at 30 years and above (Table–6.9) while the average fertility in the population was 3.30 ± 1.86 with 95% CI of 3.12–3.48. Here, the variation in the average fertility was observed to be highly significant with the women's age at first delivery as revealed by the F-Statistics, 6.29 ($P<0.01$). The pattern of the variation might perhaps be associated with age at marriage and desire of children. Besides, the practice of effective contraceptive and permanent method seems to link with the desire number of children in the latter part of their reproductive span in the population.

6.10 Fertility and Child Mortality

The present section examines the variation in the average fertility according to the mortality status of the children ever born to the mothers under study. A good number of past findings highlighted that the infant and child mortality have considerable impacts on fertility indices (Singh, 2002; Singh et al., 2007; Singh et al., 2012). Chakraborty et al., (1996) reveal that infant and child mortality have significant impact on the subsequent duration of waiting time to conception for social and biological reasons. As the major component of a closed inter live birth interval, waiting time to conception has a significant role in the fertility dynamics. Baschieri et al., (2007) also observes that risk of conception increases by 20% when first child is alive comparing with the death of the first child. Singh et al., (2007) in their empirical study, observe that the death of previous child during infancy gives significant contribution in reducing waiting time to conception after adjustment of the effects of other explanatory variables. It is again supported by the findings of Singh et al. (2010).In this analysis, the eligible women have been categorized into three groups according the number of children born alive but now deceased to a woman.

Table–6.10
Fertility differential according to number of children born alive but now deceased to a woman

No. of children	No. of house-holds (in %)	Mean ± S.D	95%CI for mean	Test values
Nil	90.2	3.00 ± 2.26	1.38–4.62	F=0.31,
One	6.6	3.16 ± 2.07	2.03–4.09	P>0.05
At least 2	3.2	3.52 ± 1.85	3.13–3.51	
Total	**100**	**3.30 ± 1.86**	**3.12–3.48**	

About 6.6% of the total mothers were found to have one child deceased at the time of survey and 3.2% mother had at least two children deceased (Table–6.10). Irrespective of the effects of other variables under analysis, the child mortality appears to affect the fertility indices in the population. While the overall mean fertility was 3.30 ± 1.86 with 95% CI: 3.12–3.48, the women who had no deceased child were found to have their fertility, 3.00 ± 2.26 with 95% CI: 1.38–4.62. The increase in fertility of 3.16 ± 2.07 with 95% CI: 2.03–4.09 was observed in the mother having one child deceased and it was alarmingly increased to 3.52 ± 1.85 with 95% CI: 3.13–3.51 of the women who had experienced at least two children deceased. The above table revealed fertility increases along with the increase in the number of deceased children, despite it was statistically insignificant.

6.11 Regression Models of Fertility

In various studies, many socio-economic and demographic factors like residence, educational status, employment, income, age at marriage, practice of family planning methods, length of birth intervals etc. have been found to influence on fertility level. In this view, a regression analysis has been carried out to the present cross-sectional data in order to explore the effects of such independent variables or predictors on fertility differential in the population. Here, the fertility level is defined as the number of live births ever born to an eligible mother. This level is assumed to be functionally related with thirteen factors, like place of residence, type of family, religion, type of latrine, source of drinking water, major means of cooking, educational level of husband, educational level of wife, family income, age at marriage of wife, number of son, number of daughter, and child mortality level. These expected causal factors are treated to be the predictor variables of interest in the regression models. To control the problem of multi-collinearity, the variables are included through scientific scanning and controlling process.

Among the above thirteen variables, age at marriage, number of son and daughter, number of deceased child, family income etc. have their quantitative values and hence at present, no difficulties of measurement. The educational level has been quantified by the number of completed years in schooling in ordinal scale (levels: 1, 2, 3, 4). The factors like place of residence, type of family, religion, type of latrine, source of drinking water, major means of cooking are obviously qualitative or categorical in nature. Thus, some suitable dichotomous dummy variables have been introduced in the analysis.

Explanatory Variable

The measurements of these variables for statistical analysis are defined as:

Response variable (Y): Fertility level (number of live birth ever born to a woman)

Predictor variables	Type	Measurement
Place of residence	Dummy	Joint=1, Others (Nuclear)=0
Type of family	Dummy	Urban=1, Others (Rural)=0
Religion	Dummy	Christian=1, Others=0
Type of latrine	Dummy	Sanitary=1, Others=0
Source of drinking water	Dummy	Pipe=1, Others (pond, river, underground etc.)=0

Major means of cooking	Dummy	Petroleum gas=1, Others=0
Educational level of husband	Quantitative	Levels: illiterate=0, literate but under matriculate=1, matriculate but below ten plus two standard=2, ten plus two standard but undergraduate=3, graduate and above=4
Educational level of wife	Quantitative	Levels: illiterate=0, literate but under matriculate=1, matriculate but below ten plus two standard=2, ten plus two standard but undergraduate=3, graduate and above=4
Family income	Quantitative	Monthly family income from all sources measured in '000 Rs
Age at marriage of wife	Quantitative	Age of wife at the time of current marriage measured in year
Number of son	Quantitative	Number of son (0,1,2,...)
Number of daughter	Quantitative	Number of daughter (0, 1, 2,...)
Child mortality level	Quantitative	Number of deceased children

Analysis and Models

Out of the above thirteen explanatory variables, only four ones were observed to have significant impacts on the fertility dynamics in the study population, the Chandel district while adjusted the joint effects of other variables under consideration. The variables were women's age at marriage (b=–0.06 with 95% CI: –0.11, –0.06) significant at 5%; number of son (b=0.57 with 95% CI: 0.33, 0.81) significant at 1% level (P<0.01); number of daughter (b=0.64 with 95% CI: 0.41, 0.87; P<0.01), and number of deceased children (–0.45 with

95% CI: –0.96, 0.05) at 5% probability level (P<0.05) (Table–6.11.1). Precisely, it might be interpreted that to each increment of one year in a woman's age at marriage, the average fertility might significantly be reduced by 0.06 children (that is one child) as evidenced by its test value (t=2.47; P<0.05) when adjusted the joint effects of the combination of other twelve factors like place of residence, type of family, religion, type of latrine, source of drinking water, major means of cooking, educational level of husband, educational level of wife, family income, number of son, number of daughter and child mortality level. In contrast, the average fertility level quantitatively as well as significantly increased by 0.57 children (i.e. one child) as per increment of one son of a couple after controlling the effects of other twelve factors under experiment (t=4.62, P<0.01). The similar effect was also witnessed in the case of number daughter too. As compared to son, the fertility response was more sensitive to the number daughter. The coefficient of the number of daughter implies that 0.64 level of fertility would increase to every increase in the number of daughter. In this study population the variation in the average fertility was found to significantly vary with child mortality. This phenomenon revealed that the average number of live birth ever born to a woman increased by 0.65 children (almost one child) corresponding to each increment of deceased child which was statistically significant (P<0.05) keeping constant the effects of other factors.

Table–6.11.1
Multiple regression analysis on fertility level

Variable	b	S.E	β	t-value	P-value	95%CI for B Lower	Upper
(Constant)	2.97	0.83		3.59	0.000	1.33	4.60
Place of residence	0.35	0.34	0.08	1.04	0.299	-0.31	1.01
Type of family	-0.49	0.53	-0.06	-0.92	0.359	-1.53	0.56
Religion of the couple	1.10	0.62	0.13	1.78	0.076	-0.12	2.31

Family Income (in '000Rs)	0.01	0.01	0.04	0.50	0.620	-0.01	0.02
Source of drinking water	-0.27	0.35	-0.05	-0.79	0.433	-0.96	0.41
Major means of cooking	-0.32	0.32	-0.07	-0.99	0.326	-0.95	0.32
Type of latrine	0.32	0.43	0.05	0.75	0.457	-0.53	1.18
Age at marriage of wife*	-0.06	0.02	-0.17	-2.47	0.015	-0.11	-0.01
Educational level of husband	-0.05	0.11	-0.04	-0.47	0.642	-0.26	0.16
Educational level of wife	-0.05	0.12	-0.03	-0.41	0.683	-0.28	0.18
No. of son**	0.57	0.12	0.32	4.62	0.000	0.33	0.81
No. of daughter**	0.64	0.12	0.37	5.46	0.000	0.41	0.87
No. of children born alive but now deceased*	0.65	0.26	0.32	2.17	0.037	0.06	0.96

* significant at 5%;

** significant at 1%

F = 7.43, P<0.001; R^2 = 0.37; Durbin-Watson Statistics = 2.00

Apart from the statistical significance, it may also be observed that the average fertility may visibly be reduced due to the advancement of educational level of the couples when adjusted the effects of other variables under consideration. Likewise, the level of practical contribution of other interested variables in the fertility dynamics may be discussed ignoring the statistical significance of the population. The model developed for the Chandel district was significant as witnessed by the F-test, 7.43 (P<0.001). The thirteen variables explained 37% of the total variations in the average fertility in the study population. The fitted regression model for the Chandel district becomes

Average number of live birth to a mother = 2.97 + 0.35 (place of residence) – 0.49(type of family) + 1.10(religion) + 0.01(family income) – 0.27(source of drinking water) – 0.27(major means of cooking) +

0.32(type of latrine) – 0.06(age at marriage of wife) – 0.05(educational level of husband) – 0.05(educational level of wife) + 0.57(number of son) + 0.64(number of daughter) + 0.65(number of children born alive but now deceased).

Categorizing the population under study into four sub-divisions viz., Tengnoupal, Machi, Chandel and Chakpikarong, separate regressions were also run for these sub-divisions. In Tengnoupal sub-division, only three explanatory variables out of the interested thirteen variables were observed to be significant predictors of the variation in the average fertility after adjusted the effects of other variables (Table–6.11.2). The predictors were educational level of wife (–0.53 ± 0.28 with 95% CI: -1.09, 0.03); number of daughter (1.15 ± 0.28 with 95% CI: 0.59, 1.71) and the number of deceased children (1.12 ± 0.44 with 95% CI: 0.61, 2.14). In the fitted regression model was significant at 1 percent (F=5.91, P<0.001) and the considered variables explained 65 percent of the total variations in the average fertility in the sub-division (Tengnoupal).

Table–6.11.2
Multiple regression analysis on fertility level in Tengnoupal sub-division

Variable	b	S.E	β	t-value	P-value	95%CI for B Lower	95%CI for B Upper
(Constant)	3.42	1.20		2.86	0.007	1.01	5.84
Place of residence	0.42	0.62	0.11	0.67	0.509	–0.85	1.68
Type of family	–0.37	1.01	–0.04	–0.37	0.716	–2.41	1.67
Religion of the couple	0.91	0.61	0.16	1.51	0.140	–0.31	2.14
Family Income (in '000Rs.)	–0.01	0.02	–0.03	–0.20	0.842	–0.04	0.03
Source of drinking water	–0.50	0.88	–0.06	–0.57	0.574	–2.27	1.28
Major means of cooking	–0.90	0.66	–0.20	–1.36	0.183	–2.24	0.44

Type of latrine	0.27	0.58	0.05	0.46	0.645	–0.88	–1.42
Age at marriage of wife	–0.06	0.04	–0.13	–1.31	0.197	–0.14	0.03
Educational level of husband	0.44	0.23	0.24	1.90	0.065	–0.03	0.90
Educational level of wife*	–0.53	0.28	–0.24	–2.19	0.044	–1.09	0.03
No. of son	0.36	0.26	0.18	1.37	0.179	–0.17	0.89
No. of daughter**	1.15	0.28	0.51	4.15	0.000	0.59	1.71
No. of children born alive but now deceased*	1.12	0.44	0.28	2.57	0.014	0.61	2.24

* significant at 5%;
** significant at 1%
F =5.91, $P < 0.001$; $R^2 = 0.65$; Durbin-Watson Statistics = 2.11

The present findings may be interpreted that to each increment of one level in educational standard of wife, the average fertility may significantly be reduced by 0.53 while adjusted the joint effects of other twelve variables place of residence, type of family, religion, type of latrine, source of drinking water, major means of cooking, educational level of husband, family income, number of son, number of daughter and child mortality level. It was evidenced by the test value, ($t=2.19$, $P<0.05$). After controlling the effects of other variables, the fertility was increased by 1.15 corresponding to each increment of one daughter to a couple ($t=4.15$, $P<0.01$). The findings also highlights that the average fertility increased by 1.12 according to each increment of deceased child which was statistically significant ($P<0.05$) keeping constant the joint effects of other factors. Thus, regression model for the Tengnoupal sub-division is given by

Average number of live birth to a mother = 3.42 + 0.42(place of residence) – 0.37(type of family) + 0.91(religion) – 0.01(family income) – 0.50(source of drinking water) – 0.90(major means of cooking) + 0.27(type of latrine) – 0.06(age at marriage of wife) + 0.44(educational level of husband) – 0.53(educational level of wife) + 0.36(number of son) + 1.15(number of daughter) + 1.12 (number of children born alive now deceased).

Out of the explanatory variables, six ones were found to be significant predictors of the changes in average fertility in Machi sub-division after adjusted the effects of the combinations of other variables (Table–6.11.3). They were type of family (–2.24 ± 1.06; P<0.05), educational level of husband (–0.43 ± 0.17; P<0.05), family income (0.05 ± 0.02; P<0.05), age at marriage of wife (–0.10 ± 0.04; P<0.05), number of son (0.54 ± 0.18; P<0.01) and the number of deceased children (1.20 ± 0.58 with 95% CI: 0.38, 2.03; P<0.05). The fitted regression model was also found to be significant (F=3.26, P<0.01) in this sub-division. The set of explanatory variables of interest explained 49 percent of the total variations in average fertility in Machi sub-division. The fitted regression model for the Machi sub-division may be observed as follows:

Average number of live birth to a mother = 7.11 – 2.24 (type of family) – 0.82(religion) + 0.05(family income) – 0.86(source of drinking water) – 0.15(major means of cooking) – 1.22(type of latrine) – 0.10(age at marriage of wife) – 0.43(educational level of husband) – 0.06(educational level of wife) + 0.54(number of son) – 0.09(number of daughter) + 1.20 (number of children born alive now deceased).

Table–6.11.3
Multiple regression analysis on fertility level of Machi sub-division

Variable	b	S.E	β	t-value	P-value	95%CI for B Lower	95%CI for B Upper
(Constant)	7.11	1.20		5.92	0.000	4.67	9.56
Type of family*	–2.24	1.06	–0.32	–2.12	0.041	–4.38	–0.10
Religion of the couple	–0.82	1.22	–0.06	–0.67	0.501	–3.23	1.59
Family Income (in '000Rs)*	0.05	0.02	0.42	2.52	0.017	0.01	0.09

Source of drinking water	–0.86	0.43	–0.27	–1.99	0.055	–1.74	0.02
Major means of cooking	–0.15	0.52	–0.04	–0.29	0.771	–1.20	0.90
Type of latrine	–1.22	0.99	–0.11	–1.22	0.224	–3.19	0.75
Age at marriage of wife*	–0.10	0.04	–0.33	–2.37	0.024	–0.19	–0.01
Educational level of husband*	–0.43	0.17	–0.35	–2.45	0.020	–0.78	–0.07
Educational level of wife	–0.06	0.18	–0.05	–0.33	0.747	–0.43	0.31
No. of son**	0.54	0.18	0.39	2.95	0.006	0.17	0.91
No. of daughter	–0.09	0.23	–0.06	–0.41	0.683	–0.56	0.37
No. of children born alive but now deceased*	1.20	0.58	0.27	2.06	0.048	0.38	2.03

* significant at 5%;
** significant at 1%
F =3.26, P <0.01; R^2 = 0.49; Durbin-Watson Statistics = 1.86

Only eleven explanatory variables were included in the regression model in Chandel sub-division. They are type of family, type of latrine, source of drinking water, major means of cooking, educational level of husband, educational level of wife, family income, age at marriage of wife, number of son, number of daughter, and child mortality level. Only two independent variables were confirmed to be significant predictors of the fertility variation in Chandel sub-division after controlling the joint effects of other variables under consideration. They were educational level of wife (–0.42 ± 0.38; P<0.05) and number of daughter (1.05 ± 0.38; P<0.05). Without considering the sense of statistical significance, the average fertility were also observed to be reduced corresponding to improvement of family income, availability of quality (pipe) water and advancement of women's age at marriage.

Table–6.11.4
Multiple regression analysis on fertility level of Chandel sub-division

Variable	b	S.E	β	t-value	P-value	95%CI for B Lower	Upper
(Constant)	3.26	1.96		1.67	0.120	–0.97	7.50
Type of family	0.15	1.20	0.03	0.12	0.905	–2.45	2.74
Family Income (in '000Rs)	–0.01	0.04	–0.10	–0.38	0.713	–0.09	0.07
Source of drinking water	–0.81	1.15	–0.16	–0.70	0.494	–3.31	1.68
Major means of cooking	0.43	0.95	0.12	0.45	0.659	–1.63	2.49
Type of latrine	0.11	0.70	0.02	0.15	0.879	–1.30	1.51
Age at marriage of wife	–0.07	0.07	–0.25	–0.91	0.378	–0.22	0.09
Educational level of husband	0.25	0.34	0.19	0.74	0.474	–0.48	0.97
Educational level of wife*	–0.42	0.38	–0.30	–2.09	0.026	–1.24	0.41
No. of son	0.63	0.62	0.25	1.03	0.323	–0.69	1.96
No. of daughter*	1.05	0.38	0.72	2.76	0.016	0.23	1.87
No. of children born alive but now deceased	0.29	0.85	0.08	0.34	0.743	–1.56	2.13

* significant at 5%

F =4.14, P <0.05; R^2 = 0.47; Durbin-Watson Statistics = 1.94

The regression model fitted in the Chandel sub-division was found to be significant, as witnessed by the model test value, F(4.14, P<0.05). In this model, 47% of the total variation in the average fertility can be explained by the eleven variables of interest in this sub-division. Precisely, the fitted model is given by the following equation.

Average number of live birth to a mother = 3.26 + 0.15 (type of family) – 0.01(family income) – 0.81(source of drinking water) + 0.43(major means of cooking)

+ 0.11(type of latrine) – 0.07(age at marriage of wife) + 0.25(educational level of husband) – 0.42 (educational level of wife) + 0.63(number of son) + 1.05(number of daughter) + 0.29 (number of children born alive now deceased).

As in the Chandel sub-division, eleven explanatory variables – type of family, type of latrine, source of drinking water, major means of cooking, educational level of husband, educational level of wife, family income, age at marriage of wife, number of son, number of daughter, and child mortality level were included in the regression analysis in Chakpikarong sub-division. Out of the interested independent variables, only three predictors were observed to be significant variables on the fertility dynamics in Chakpikarong sub-division after controlling the joint effects of other variables. The predictors were source of drinking water (–1.36 ± 1.09 with 95% CI: –2.15, 0.57), number of son (0.64 ± 0.21 with 95% CI: 0.21–1.07) and number of daughter (0.70 ± 0.19). While adjusted the joint effects of other remaining variables the average fertility might significantly be reduced by 1.36 if the couple gets the pipe drinking water. It was evidenced by the test value, ($t=2.17, P<0.05$). Availability of pipe water might mean that people of that area are more conscious about health of children (that is quality of children). In this sub-division, the average fertility increased corresponding to the number of children (sons and daughters) to the couple (son: $t=3.01, P<0.01$ and daughter: $t=3.61, P<0.01$) after adjusted the joint effects of other factors under consideration.

Table–6.11.5

Multiple regression analysis on fertility level in Chakpikarong sub-division

Variable	b	S.E	β	t-value	P-value	95%CI for B Lower	Upper
(Constant)	3.08	1.34		2.30	0.027	0.36	5.81
Type of family	–1.08	0.95	–0.13	–1.13	0.266	–3.01	0.86

Family Income (in '000Rs)	0.01	0.01	0.16	1.30	0.201	–0.01	0.04
Source of drinking water*	–1.36	1.09	–0.28	–2.17	0.037	–2.15	0.57
Major means of cooking	–0.37	0.66	–0.07	–0.55	0.586	–1.71	0.98
Type of latrine	0.12	0.59	0.03	0.75	0.777	–1.01	1.36
Age at marriage of wife	–0.06	0.05	–0.15	–1.25	0.220	–0.15	0.04
Educational level of husband	–0.30	0.19	–0.23	–1.59	0.121	–0.68	0.08
Educational level of wife	0.13	0.19	0.09	0.67	0.505	–0.26	0.51
No. of son**	0.64	0.21	0.36	3.01	0.005	0.21	1.07
No. of daughter**	0.70	0.19	0.44	3.61	0.001	0.30	1.09
No. of children born alive but now deceased	0.15	0.43	0.04	0.36	0.725	–0.73	1.03

* significant at 5 percent;

** significant at 1 percent

$F = 4.43$, $P < 0.001$; $R^2 = 0.56$; Durbin-Watson Statistics = 2.08

The positive Signof child ever born (i.e. both number of son and daughter) might mean that they do not bother much about higher number of child considering their socio-economic environment (Table–6.11.5). Apart from statistical significance, the average fertility were also observed to be reduced corresponding to availability of petroleum gas as the major means of cooking in the family, advancement of women's age at marriage and educational level of husband in the sub-division. The fitted regression model in the sub-division was also found to be significant ($F=4.43$, $P<0.001$). Here, 56% of the total variation in average fertility was explained by the eleven variables of interest in Chapikarong sub-division. The regression model developed may be expressed by the equation.

Average number of live birth to a mother = 3.08 – 1.08 (type of family) + 0.01 (family income) – 1.36 (source of drinking water) – 0.37 (major means of cooking) + 0.12 (type of latrine) – 0.06 (age at marriage of wife) – 0.30 (educational level of husband) + 0.13 (educational level of wife) + 0.64 (number of son) + 0.70 (number of daughter) + 0.15 (number of children born alive now deceased).

Discussion

Irrespective of the effects of other variables, the variation in the average fertility is observed to be significantly varied with a few independent variables like different community (tribes), employment status of the eligible couple, age at marriage, and age at first delivery in the above bivariate analysis. The regression analysis reveals that in Chandel district the significant explanatory variables in explaining the variation of human fertility were age at marriage of wife, number of sons, number of daughter and child mortality. The significant explanatory variables in all four sub-divisions were not the same due to various factors including socio-economic factors. Number of sons, child mortality, type of family, educational level of husband, family income and women age at marriage were significant in Machi sub-division, while number of sons, number of daughter and source of drinking water in Chakpikarong, number of daughter, child mortality and educational level of wife in Tengnoupal and number of daughter and educational level of wife in Chandel sub-divison were significant. The finding highlighted that as the number of deceased children increases the number of live birth tends to be increased owing to the fact that the couples like to compensate the loss children at any cost. This view is supported by the findings of Hossain et al., (2006), Bascheiri et al., (2007), Singh et al., (2007), Singh et al., (2012). After adjusted the joint effects of other variables the dynamics in the average fertility has linkage with the number of daughter to a couple which may perhaps be due to unavoidable problems of son preference causing high fertility in the population. At the same time, many past findings also highlighted that India is known to have strong son preference (Bhat and Zavier 2003; Pande and Astone 2007, Singh et al., 2011). The similar views have been directly or indirectly in agreement with other findings of the studies conducted in many parts of the globe (Yount et al., 2000; Vignoli, 2006). Many Scholars have observed son preference in India through sex-selective abortions that lead to abnormally high sex ratios at birth (Arnold et al., 2002), differential fertility and contraceptive use behavior (Clark, 2000; Arokiasamy, 2002), female disadvantage in juvenile mortality (Gupta and Bhat, 1997), and gender bias in the allocation of food and health care (Retherford, 2004).

The women's age at marriage had negative impact on fertility which was highly significant in the present analysis. This leads us to the conclusion that by rising age at marriage of wife, the average fertility can be brought down. The higher age at marriage is observed among those who are belonging to the higher income group and higher age at marriage shortens the reproductive spans which, in turn, reduce the fertility level. On the other hand, education depresses fertility by rising the age at marriage, strengthening the propensity to be in the labour force, fostering a favourable attitude towards small family norm and improving awareness and use of family planning methods. This view is incorporated with the findings of the studies conducted by Castertine (1983); Das and Dey (1998); Harvindar (2000); Yadav et al., (2000); Sheela and Audinarayana (2000), Singh et al., (2007); Singh et al., (2010); Palamuleni (2011) and Nath et al., (2012).

7

Chapter

Summary

Many studies have examined the impact of economic development as socio economic variables but a few economists have attempted to find out the influences of socio-economic variables on economic development. Moreover, these studies also pertain to economics other than hilly regions. On this background the present study has examined the impact of socio-economic factors on the economic development of Chandel which is one of hill districts of Manipur.

This study has provided quantitative estimates of the coefficient of socio-economic variables and tested the relevant hypothesis regarding the influence of socio-economic variables on the economic development. This relation has been examined throw growth of income level, agricultural production and human fertility. The influence of socio-economic variables on these three dependent variables has been analysed. For analysing these relation data were collected from the primary source. The primary data was collected from 1071 households in Chandel district of Manipur by using stratified random sampling. The collected data are analysed with the help of descriptive statistics and classical regression analysis through SPSS vs 23. Analysis has been done not only for Chandel district but also been performed for four sub-divisions of the district namely, Chakpikarong, Machi, Chandel and Tengnoupal. The relevant findings are provided as below:

The family income differential of the study population according to eighteen socio-economic variables has been analysed with descriptive statistics- means, standard deviation, t-test and F- test. Among these variables, income differential according to sub-division, number of literate family member, number of male literate family member, educational level of male spouse and number of agricultural workers are found significant. In addition to these descriptive analyses, the causal relation has been examined through regression analysis. Among the explanatory variables for family income variation, area under rice cultivation, number of family members engaged in agricultural activities, number of literate person, educational status of male spouse and number of live birth ever born to a woman are found to be statistically significant. The first and last variables are significant at 10% and remaining three at 1%.

This study has also examined impact of socio-economic factors on rice production which is very crucial for economic development of the tribal district. Factors affecting rice production has been analysed through two types of cultivation methods – wet cultivation and shifting cultivation. The socio-economic variables included are area under rice cultivations, number of male agricultural worker, number of literate persons in the family, irrigation facility, labour cost, cost of chemical fertiliser, cost of pesticides, cost of insecticides, cost of bullock/tractor and size of family. At district, the regression analysis shows that among these socio-economic variables, area under rice cultivations and irrigations facility have been found significant at 1% in wet cultivation method. But paradoxically area under rice cultivation has negative impact on rice production. This might be due to negligence of farmers who extend the area of cultivation under his control.

Further analysis was made for four-divisions of Chandel district. In Machi sub-division area under rice cultivation, irrigation facility and cost of chemical fertiliser are found significant in explaining rice production. But like area, cost of fertilisers paradoxically has positive sign. This unexpected sign of cost of fertilizers can be explained in such a way that when cost of fertilizer increases, farmers might be more conscious about proper using of these inputs (in terms of proper combination of nutrients of chemical fertilizers, timely using and applying of these nutrients according to breeds and soil).

However, further investigation is call for. In Tengnoupal only irrigation variable has been found significant at 1%. In the case of Chandel sub-division irrigation facility and cost of labour have been found significant at 1% and 5% level respectively. The sign of cost of labour has unexpected (positive) sign. This might be due to substitution effect. When price of labour increases labour is substituted by other factors of productions having lower prices and/or higher efficiencies. In the case of Chakpikarong sub-division the significant explanatory socio-economic variables are number of female worker and irrigation facility. These variables are significant at 5%.

The models under shifting-cultivation reveal that only three variables – area under rice cultivation, jhum cycle and labour cost are found significant in explaining the variation in rice production in Chandel district. The statistical level of significances of the former two are at 1% and that of last variable is at 5%. The sign of area under rice cultivation and cost of labour are contrary to common belief. The analysis on the impact of socio-economic variables on rice production in the four sub-divisions shows that area under rice cultivation, Jhum cycle, number of female labour and labour cost in Machi sub-division; Jhum cycle and number of literate family member in Tengnoupal; area under rice cultivation, jhum cycle, labour cost in Chandel and area under rice cultivation and Jhum cycle in Chakpikarong are found significant at different levels. The signs of area under rice cultivation (in all sub-divisions), labour cost (in Machi and Chandel sub-divisions) and number of literates in the family (in Tengnoupal sub-division) are paradoxical to common belief. The possible reasons of the former two have been explained above. In the case of the sign of literates, the plausible reason is the work culture of literate persons in this hill district.

The bivariate study in chapter-six has provided strong evidence in favour of the hypothesis that variation in the average fertility is influenced by socio-economic variables like community, employment status, age at marriage and age at first delivery. Regression study has also demonstrated that four socio-economic variables–women's age at marriage, number of son, number of daughter and number of deceased children significantly influence the variation in fertility in Chandel district. Sub-divisional analyses were also made. In Tengnoupal sub-division, the change in fertility has significantly been influenced by educational level of wife, number of daughter and number of children born alive but now deceased. In the case of Machi, the significant socio-economic factors which explain the change in fertility are type of family, family income, age at marriage of wife, educational level of husband, number of son and number of children born alive but now deceased. The multiple regression coefficients which are significant in explaining the fertility variation were educational level of wife and number of daughter in Chandel sub-division. The three important explanatory variables of this dependent variable were source of drinking water, number of son and number of daughter in Chakpikarong sub-division. The explanatory or independent variables which are found significant in explaining the variation in human fertility level in Chandel district and its sub-divisions include women's age at marriage, number of son, number of daughter, child mortality, educational level of wife and husband, type of family, income, and source of drinking water.

The findings of the present study indicate that socio-economic variables can be effective devices for increasing per capita income or economic development of this district in particular and north-eastern in general. Further, this study implies that socio-economic policies can meaningfully influence the level of income, rice production and human fertility for achieving economic development of tribal society as well as north eastern-region having the characteristics of Chandel district in general. To achieve higher growth rate income, priorities of government policy may be given to the removal of illiteracy, the elevation of educational level of spouses and the reduction of human fertility. Among the determinants of agricultural production, irrigation is the most important variables in the case of wet-cultivation and raising jhum cycle is the most significant factor in the case of shifting cultivation. Thus providing irrigation facilities and raising jhum cycle may be the top priorities in the hill area in general and Chandel district in particular. Emphasis of government policies on educational level is highly necessary for reducing human fertility which is attainable particularly through higher female age at marriage and awareness of population control. Further, the findings of present study clearly indicate the importance of providing government job opportunities and reduction of infant and child mortality for reducing human fertility.

Though the scope of this study has been restricted to Chandel district, the results are applicable in many areas having the similar socio-economic characteristics. The results may be different in any tribal areas of the country but it is believed that the results would not very much different from what are found here. However, it is matter for further investigation for getting better understanding and precise result of socio-economic variables in the particular area.The approach undertaken in this study may be replicated in other areas, particularly north-eastern region and other hilly region of the country where the standard of living and culture of these people are not much different from that of Chandel district. The unexpected negative sign of area under investigation to explain the variation in agricultural production and positive sign of impact of labour cost and cost of fertiliser on agricultural production are also required to investigate further.

Bibliography

Abhimanya, K., 2012. "Religion visa vis Fertility and Family Planning Behaviour in Uttar Pradesh, India", Journal of Research in Peace, Gender and Development 2(1): 10-21.

Acemoglu, D. and Joshua, A., 2001, "How Large are Human-Capital Externalities Evidence from Compulsory-Schooling Laws in NBER Macro-economics Annual 2000", Vol. 15, htttp://www. Nber.org/book/bern 01-1.

Adhikari, R., 2010, "Demographic, Socio-Economic, and Cultural Factors Affecting Fertility Differentials in Nepal", BMC Pregnancy and Child birth: 10-19 http://biomed central.com/1471-393.

Adler, N., 1994, "Socio-economic Status and Health: The Change of the Gradient", American Psychologist, 49(1): 15-24.

Akman, W., 2002, "Woman's Education and Fertility Rates in Developing Countries with special reference to Bangladesh", Eubios Journal of Asian and International Bioethics, 12: 138-143.

Alam, Md. M., Chamhuri, S., Basri, T. and Mohd, E. T., 2011, "The Relationship Between the Socio-Economic Profiles of Farmers and Paddy Productivity in North-West Selangor", Malyasia Asia Pacific Development Journal 18(1).

Alemayehu, Z. Y., 2017, "Assessing Determinants of Population Fertility in Hosanna Town", South Ethiopia. Journal of Health and Environmental Research. 3(2): 22-26.

Anand, S. and Harris, C., 1994, "Choosing a Welfare Indicator", American Economic Review, 84: 226 -231.

Anigbogu, T. U., Objanuju, E. A. and Ikechukwu, M. O., 2015, "Socio-Economic Factors Influencing Agricultural Production among Co-operative Farmers in Anamba State, Nigeria", International Journal of Academic Research in Economics and Management Sciences, 1(3): 2226-3624.

Arnold, F., Sunita, K. and Roy, T. K., 2002, "Sex Selective Abortions in India", Population and Development Review, 28: 759-785.

Arokiasamy, P., 2002, "Gender Preference Contraception Use and Fertility in India", Regional and Development Influences, International Journal of Population Geography, 8: 49-67.

Aturupane, H. Glewwe, P. and Isenman, P., 1994, "Poverty, Human Development, and Growth: An Emerging Consensus?", American Economic Review, 84: 224-249.

Awad, A. and Yussof, I., 2017, "Factors Affecting Fertility-New Evidence from Malaysia", In: Chodlkowska, M. J. and Szymanska, D. (Eds) Bulletin of Geography, Socio Economic Serials, 36: 7-20.

Barman. R. N. and Das, R., 2010, "A Study of Socio-Economic Factors Influencing Adoption of Farm Level Soil and Water Conservation Practices in the Riverine of North Bank Plains Zone of Assam", Indian Journal of Agricultural Economics, 65(3): 439-447.

Barro, R. J., 1996, "Determinants of Economic Growth: A Cross-Country Empirical Study", NBER Working Paper 5698, National Bureau of Economic Research, 1050, Massachusetts Avenue Cambridge, MA 02138.

Barro, R. J., 2013, "Education and Economic Growth", Annals of Economic and Finance, 14(2A): 277-304.

Barro, R. J. and Lee, J. W., 2001, "Human Capital and Growth", American Economic Review, 91(2): 12-17

Baschieri, A. and Hinde, A., 2007, "The Proximate

Determinants of Fertility and Birth Interval in Egypt: An Application of Calendar Data", Demographic Research, 16(3): 59-96.

Basu, K., 2000, "Analytical Development Economics – The Less Developed Economy Revisited", Oxford University Press, New Delhi: 45.

Becker, G. S., 1960, "An economic Analysis of Fertility in Demographic and Economic Change in Developing Countries" – National Bureau Conference, Series No. 11, Princeton, N. J. Princeton University Press, 1960: 209-231.

Becker, G. S., 1994, Human Capital Revisited in Human Capital: A Theoretical and Empirical Analysis with Special Reference to Education: 15-28. http://www.nber.org/chapters/c11229.

Bhagat, R. B. and Chattopadhyay, A., 2004, "Characteristics and Correlates of Tribal Fertility: A Comparative Study of Selected Tribes Demography India", 33(2): 295-310.

Bhagat, R. B. and Chattopadhyay, A., 2004, "Characteristics and Correlates of Tribal Fertility: A Comparative Study of Selected Tribes. Demography India", 33(2): 295-310.

Bhat, P. N. and Zavier, A. J., 2003, "Fertility Decline any Gender bias in Northern India", Demography, 40: 637-657.

Bongaarts, J., 1978, "A framework for Analyzing the Proximate Determinants of Fertility", Population and Development Review, Population Council 4(1): 105-131.

Borg, M. M., 1989, "The Income – Fertility Relationship: Effect of the Net Price of a Child", Demography, 26(2): 301-310.

Breschi, M., Alessio, F., Matteo, M., Lucra, P., Rosella, R. and Francesco, S., 2014, "Social and Economic Determinants of Reproductive Behaviour before the Fertility Decline", European Journal of Populations, 30(3): 291-315.

Chadha, G. K., 2003, "Indian Agriculture in the New Millennium: Human Response to Technology Challenges", Indian Journal of Agricultural Economics, 1(58): 1-31.

Chakraborty, N., Sharmin, S. and Islam, M. A., 1996, "Differential pattern of birth Interval is Bangladesh", Asia Pacific Population Journal, 11 (4): 73-86.

Chandiok, K., Prakash, R. M., Chakravarty, M. and Kallur, N. S., 2016, "Biological and Social Development of Fertility Among the Jat Women of Haryana State, India", Journal of Anthropology, https://doi.org/10.1155/2016/5463168.

Chani, M. I., Muhammad, S. M. and Hassan, V. I., 2012, "Some Socio-Economic Determinants of Fertility in Pakistan: an Empirical Analysis", National College of Business Administration and Economics, Lahore, Pakistan, Health and Nutrition Supervisor, Health Department, Government of Punjab, Sheikhupura, Pakistan. MPRA Paper No. 38742: 3-12.

Choe, M. K. Thapa, S. and Mishra, V., 2005, "Early Marriage and Early Motherhood in Nepal", Journal of Biosocial Science, 37(21): 143-162.

Christenson, B. A. and Nan, E. J., 1995, "Educational Inequality in Adults Mortality: Assessment with Death Certificate Date in Michigan", Demography, 32: 215-230.

Clark, S., 2000, "Son Preference and Sex Composition of Children: Evidence from India", Demography, 37: 95-108.

D'Souza, G., Douglas, C. and Tim, Phipps, 1993, "Factors Affecting the Adoption of Sustainable Agricultural practices", Agricultural and Resource Economic Review, October: 159-165.

Das, N. P. and Dey, D., 1998, "Female Age at Marriage in India: Trends and Determinants", Demography India, 27 (1): 109-115.

Das, N. P. and Dey, D., 2003, "Understanding the causative Factors behind Stalling of Infant Mortality in India", Demography India, 32 (2): 249-274.

Desai, M., 1991, "Human Development: Concepts and Measurement", European Economic Review, 35: 350-357.

Dreze, J. and Mamta, M., 1999, "Fertility, Education and

Development: Further Evidence from India", www.histe.com, Magd.com.ac.uk, November, 22.

Dribe, M., Marco, B. and Alain, G., 2016, "Socio-Economic Status and Fertility declined: Insights from Historical Transition in Europe and North America", Population Studies, 71(1): 3-21.

Dribe, M., Oris, M. and Possi, L., 2014, "Socio-Economic Status and Fertility Before, During and After the Demographic Transition", Demographic Research, 31(7): 161-192.

Easterlin, R. A., 1969, "Towards a Socio-Economic Theory of Fertility: A Survey of Recent Research on Economic Factors, In American Fertility, In fertility and Family Planning: A World View" (Ed.) S.J. Behrman, Leslie Corsa, Jr and Ronald Freeman Ann Abor; Michigan University Press: 127-155.

Easterline, R. A., 1967, "The Effect of Population Growth on the Economic Developing Countries", The Annals of the American Academy of Polity, 98-108.

Elo, I. T. and Samual, H. P., 1992, "Effects of Early Life Condition in Adult Mortality: a Review", Population Index 58(2): 186-212.

Ester, B., 1965, "The conditions of Agricultural Growth", "The economics of Agrarian Change under Population Pressure", London George Allen and Unwin Ltd. Ruskin House museum Street.

Ghannam, R. E., 2005, "An Examination of Factors Affecting Fertility Rate Differentials as Compared among Women in Less and More Developed Countries", Department of Rural Sociology, Agricultural Extension and Rural Development Research Institute, Agriculture Research Centre, Egypt: 181-184.

Gupta, D. M. and Bhat, P. N., 1997, "Fertility Decline and Increased Manifestation of Sec bias in India", Population Studies 51: 307-315.

Harvinder, K., 2000, "Impact of Income and Education on Fertility", The Journal of Family Welfare, 46 (1): 70-76.

Heaton, T. B., 1996, "Socio-Economic and Familial Status of Women Associated with Age at First Marriage in Three Stamic Societies", Journal of Comparative Family Studies 27(1): 41-58.

Hossain, M. B., Phillips, J. F. and LeGrand, A., 2006, "The Impact of Childhood Mortality on Fertility in Six Rural Thanas of Bangladesh, Policy Research Division, New York Working Paper, 198: 1-14.

Hummer, R., 1998, "Socio-Demographic Differential in Adult Mortality: a Review of Analytic Approaches", Population and Development Review, 24(3): 553-578.

James, K. S., 1999, "Fertility Decline in Andhra Pradesh – A Search for Alternative Hypotheses", Economic and Political Weekly, Working Paper 20: 491-499.

Kelley, A. C., 1988, "Economic Consequences of Population Changes in the Third World", Journal of Economic Literature, 26(4): 1685-1728.

Khan, T. and Rane E. K., 2010, "Fertility Behaviour of Women and their Household Characteristics: A Case-Study of Punjab, Pakistan", Journal of Human Economics, 30 (1): 11-17.

Koenig, M. A. Phillips, J., Champbell, O. M. and D'Souza, S., 1990, "Birth Intervals and Childhood Mortality in Rural Bangladesh", Demography, 27(2): 251-265.

Kreyenfeld, M. and Gunner, A., 2014, "Socio-Economic Difference in the Unemployment and Fertility nexus", Evidence from Denmark and Germany, Advances in Life Course Research, 21: 59-73.

Kumar, A., Keshav Prasad, R. R., Rajput, M. M. and Sachan, B. S., 2010, "Determinants Influencing the Acceptance of Resource Conservation Technology: Case of Zero-Tillage in Rice-Wheat Farming systems in Uttar Pradesh, Bihar and Haryana States", Indian Journal of Agricultural Economics, 65(3): 448-460.

Kumar, G. A. and Danabalam, M., 2006, "Determinants of Delayed first Birth", Indian Journal of Community Medicine, 31(4): 10-12.

Mahadevan, K., 1979, "Sociology of Fertility: Determinants of Fertility Differentials in South India", Staling Publishers, New Delhi.

Martin, D., Michel, O. and Lucia, P., 2014, "Socio-Economic Status and Fertility Before, During, and After the Demographic Transition: An Introduction", Demographic Research, 31(7): 161-182.

Martin, T. C., 1995, "Women's Education and Fertility: Results from twenty six Demographic and Health Surveys", Studies in Family Planning, 26: 187-202.

Maubrigades, S., 2015, "Connection between Women's Age at Marriage and Social and Economic Development", Programe de Historia Economics Y Social-Unidad Multi disciplineria Documents on Line No-39, Julio, http://ideas, repec.org>udc>doctra.

Mohanty, S. K., Guenther, F., Rajesh, K. C. and David, C., 2015, "Distal Determinants of Fertility Decline", Evidence from 640 Indian Districts, May, Working Paper No. 129, Program on the Global Demography of Aging at Harvard University.

Muthi, M., Anne-Catherine, G. and Jean, D., 1995, "Mortality, Fertility and Gender Bias in India: A District level Analysis", Population and Development Review, 21(4): 745-752.

Nagarajan, R., Aurora, A. C. and Teixeira, S., 2013, "The Impact of an Ageing Population on Economic Growth: An Exploratory Review of the Main Mechanisms", FEP Working Papers 504, September.

Nahar, L. and Rahman, M., 2006, "Changes in Socio-Economic differentials of Age at Marriage and First Birth during 1983-1994 in Matlab, Bangladesh", Demography India, 35(1): 1-14.

Nanda, S., 2005, "Cultural Determinants of Human Fertility:

A study of Tribal Population in Orissa", Anthropologist, 7(3): 221-227.

Naqvi, S. N., 1995, "The Nature of Economic Development. World Development", 23: 543-556.

Nath, D. C. and Deka, A. K., 2004, "The Importance of Son in a Traditional Society: How Elderly Parents see it?", Demography India, 33(1): 33-46.

Nath, D. C., Singh, N. S. and Singh, H. B., 2012, "Fertility Transition through Four Generations and Determinants of Third Birth in Manipur", Janshamkhya' 32(2), 17-22.

Nwibo, S. U and Alimba, J. O., 2013, "Determinants of Investment Decisions among Agribusiness Investors in South-East, Nigeria", Journal of Business Management, 8(6): 60-67.

Obasi, P. C., Henri-Ukoha, A., Ukewuihe, I. S. and Chidiebere, N. M., 2013, "Factors Affecting Agricultural Productivity among Arable Crop Farmers in Imo State, Nigeria", American Journal of Experimented Agriculture, 3(2): 443-454.

Palamuleni, M. E., 2011, "Socio-Economic Determinants of Age at marriage in Malawi", International Journal of Sociology and Anthropology, 3(7): 224-235.

Pande, R. and Astone, N. M., 2001, "Explaining son preference in rural India: The independent role of structural vs. individual factors", Annual Meeting of the Population Association of America, Washington DC.

Pande, R. P. and Astone, N. M., 2007, "Explaining Son Preference in Rural India: The Independent Role of Structural versus Individual Factors", Population Research and Policy Review, 26(1): 1-29.

Patnaik, M. M., 1985, "Fertility Behaviour", Janaki Publications, New Delhi.

Pegkas, P., 2014, "The Link between Educational Levels and Economic Growth: A Neoclassical Approach for the Case of Greece, Pegkas", International Journal of Applied Economics, 11(2): 38-54.

Peterson, E. W., 2017, "The Role of Population in Economic Growth", www.journals.sage.pub.com/doi/abs:1-15.

Prachuabonob, V., 2005, "Southeast Asia's population in a changing Asian Context: Policy Implications", [Accessed 2005, Aug 12] Available from URL: http://www.jussp.org/Bangladesh2002/5APPL.

Rajaretnam, T., 1990, "How Delaying Marriage and Spacing Birth Contribution to Population Control: An Explanation with Illustrations", The Journal of Family Welfare, 36(4): 3-13.

Ramasamy, C., Paramasivam, P. and Keijiro, O., 1902, "Modern Seed Fertiliser Technologies and Adoption of Labour Saving Technology in Rice Production: The Tamil Nadu Case", Indian Journal of Agriculture Economics, 1(47): 90-107.

Rao, C. A., 2003, "Measuring and Explaining Technical Efficiency in Crop Production in Andhra Pradesh, Indian", Journal of Agricultural Economics 4(58): 768-780.

Rao, V., 1997, "Wife-Beating in Rural South India: A Qualitative and Economic Analysis", Social Science and Medicine, 44(8): 1169-1180.

Ray, D., 2001, "Development Economics", Oxford University Press, New Delhi: 330.

Retherford, R. D. and Choe, M. K., 1998, "Statistical Models for Causal Analysis", A Willy-Inter Science Publication: 38-40.

Romer, M. P., 1990, "Endogenous Technological Change", Journal of Political Economy, 38(5): 71-102.

Rop, A. K., 1992, "Socio-Economic Determinants of Fertility: What do we know?", Demography India, 21 (1): 19-28.

Rosenzweig, M. R., 1987, "Human Capital, Population Growth and Economics Development: Beyond Correlation, Economics Development Centre Development of Economics Minneapolis, Department of Agricultural and Applied Economics", St. Paul. University of Minnesota, Bulletin No 87-8, July.

Roy, B. C. and Suresh, P., 2002, "Investment, Agricultural Productivity and Rural Poverty in India: A State-Level Analysis", Indian Journal of Agricultural Economics, 4(57): 653-678.

Roy, T. K., Jayachandran, V. and Benerjee, S. K., 1999, "Economic Condition and Fertility: Is There a Relationship", Economic and Political Weekly, Oct 16-23: 3041-3046.

Saha, K. B. and Verma, 2006, "High Fertility among Scheduled Tribes of Madhya Pradesh", Indian Journal of Medical Research, 123: 89-90.

Salahuddin, M. Rabiul, I. and Syed, A. S., 2009, "Determinants of Environment in Muslim Developing Countries: An Empirical Investigation", International Journal of Economic and Management, 3(1): 100-129.

Sarker, S., Arifuzzaman, K., Mehdad, M. M., 2016, "Urban Population and Economic Growth", South Asia Perspective, 5(1): 1-12.

Savitri, R., 1994, "Fertility Decline in Tamil Nadu-Some Issues", Economic and Political Weekly, 16: 1850-1852.

Shawky, S. and Milaat, W., 2001, "Cumulative Impact of Early Maternal Marital Age during the Childhood Period", Paediatric and Perinatal Epidemiology, 15 (1): 27-33.

Sheela, J. and Audinarayana, N., 2000, "Determinants of Female Age at First Marriage in Tamil Nadu: An Analysis of NFHS Data", Journal of Family Influence on Family Planning Behaviour among Non-Adopters, Journal of Family Welfare, 30(4): 92-101.

Siddiqui, R., 1960, "The Impact of Socio-Economic Factors on Fertility Behaviour: A Cross-Country Analysis", The Pakistan Development Review, 35(2): 107-128.

Singh, N. S., 2002, "A Contribution to Determinants of Birth Interval and Fertility of Manipuri Women: A Case Study of Imphal", Ph. D. Thesis (unpublished), Manipur University, Imphal.

Singh, N. S., Narendra, R. K. and Hemochandra, L., 2007,

"Determinants of Waiting Time to Conception in Manipuri Women", Kuwait Medical Journal, 39(1): 39-43.

Singh, N. S., Singh, N. S. and Narendra, R. K., 2011, "Survival Analysis of Duration of Waiting Time to Conception", Electronic Journal of Applied Statistical Application, 4(2): 144-154.

Singh, S. N., Singh, N. S. and Narendra, R. K., 2010, "Demographic and Socio-Economic Determinants of Birth Interval Dynamics in Manipur: A survival Analysis", Journal Health and Allied Sciences, 9(4): 3-10.

Siow, L. L., 2014, "Socio-Economic and Proximate Determinants of Fertility in the Philippines", World Applied Sciences Journal, 31(10): 1828-1836.

Srivivasan , T. N., 1994, "Human Development: A New paradigm or Reinvention of the Wheel", American Economic Review, 84(2): 238-243.

Streeten, P. P., 1994, "Human Development: Means and Ends", American Economic Review, 84(3): 232-237.

Teachman, J. D. and Heckert, D. A., 1985, "The Declining Significance of First Birth Timing", Demography, 22(2): 185-198.

Timothy, O. R. and Krishnamoorthy, S., 1990, "Productivity Variation and Water Use in Farms of Madurantakam Tank fed Area of Chengalpattu District, Tamil Nadu", Indian Journal of Agricultural Economics, 1(XLV): 56-60.

Tripathy, T., Steve, H. and Bimal, K. M., 2006, "Trend of Production, Adoption and Utilisation of High Quality Paddy Seeds: A Study in Orissa", Indian Journal of Agricultural Economics, 61(1): 90-107.

Vignoli, D., 2006, "Fertility Change in Egypt: From Fertility to Third Birth", MPIDR Working Paper, 2006-2011.

Yadava, N. S., Jain, S. K. and Kumar, A., 2000, "Fertility Differentials in Eastern Utter Pradesh: A Multivariate Analysis", Janasamkhya 18: 18-29.

Yount, K. M., Langsten, R. and Hill, K., 2000, "The Effects of

Gender Preference on contraception use and facility in rural Egypt", Studies in Family Planning, 31 (4): 290-300.

Yurtseven, C., 2015, "The Socio-Economic Determinants of Fertility Rates in Muslim Countries: A Dynamic Panel Data Analysis", Economics and Sociology, 8(4): 165-178.

Zheng, Z., 2000, "Social-Demographic Influence on First Birth Interval in China, 1980-1992", Journal of Biosocial Sciences, 32(3): 315-327.